THE
BURRITO
BOOK

THE
BURRITO
BOOK

P.J. BIROSIK

AVON BOOKS ◆ NEW YORK

''South African Burrito'' recipe on p. 56 was adapted from a recipe in *African News Cookbook* by Tami Hultman. Copyright © 1985 by Africa News Service, Inc. Used by permission of Viking Penguin, a division of Penguin Books USA, Inc.

THE BURRITO BOOK is an original publication of Avon Books. This work has never before appeared in book form.

AVON BOOKS
A division of
The Hearst Corporation
1350 Avenue of the Americas
New York, New York 10019

Copyright © 1991 by P.J. Birosik
Cover illustration by Tom Nikosey
Interior art by Jeanne Richmond
Published by arrangement with the author
Library of Congress Catalog Card Number: 91-21880
ISBN: 0-380-76428-8

Library of Congress Cataloging in Publication Data:

Birosik, Patti Jean.
  The burrito book / P.J. Birosik.
    p.   cm.
1. Burritos (Cookery)   I. Title.
TX836.B57 1991   91-21880
641.5972—dc20   CIP

First Avon Books Trade Printing: October 1991

AVON TRADEMARK REG. U.S. PAT. OFF. AND IN OTHER COUNTRIES, MARCA REGISTRADA, HECHO EN U.S.A.

Printed in the U.S.A.

ARC   10 9 8 7 6 5 4 3 2 1

I'd like to thank my always supportive (and a joy to talk to) agent, Madeleine Morel; my untiring and inspiring editor, Bob Mecoy; the Avon Books executive and sales staff for making me feel so at home during their sojourn to Scottsdale; my family and friends for putting up with the long hours and absences; and Larry, for doing the dishes!

Contents

PREFACE

▼ ▼ ▼

Sitting here in the pure, still air at 4,500 feet, surrounded by majestic cypresses and sycamores, looking over my computer screen at the deep red Navajo sandstone formations that form the heart of the coyote-baying, soulful Southwest, I am reminded of one thing—that cooking conditions change.

Suffice it to say that while making burritos is not an exact science, you may still have to make adjustments in these recipes. For while a rose is a rose is a rose, a medium tomato is not necessarily medium because of differences in weight or ripeness. Similarly, chili peppers can be inexplicably incendiary one season and merely hot the next. So try your hand at the mouth-watering morsels included in this book as they are, then adjust according to taste. There is no wrong way to make a burrito, but some sure do taste better than others.

Also, don't be afraid to experiment. There is a fun side to making burritos. If Anaheim chilies don't tickle your fancy, maybe jalapeños will! The main thing to remember is that the best burrito is a perfect amalgam of sauce (salsa or mole) and ''dry'' ingredients (meat, beans, grains, etc.) heated (or chilled) to the optimum temperature.

If you need to seek further inspiration, look at a few of the Mexican cookbooks in your local library. Burritos can be a feast in themselves, but when creating a banquet, other compatible dishes are necessary. That's when enchiladas, fajitas, quesadillas, and other Southwestern delights become admirable appetite whetters to the pièce de résistance—the gourmet burrito! Enjoy, have fun, and be creative! Vivo burrito!

INTRODUCTION

▼ ▼ ▼

Millions of people are discovering the joys of the no-longer humble burrito. Forget Humphrey Bogart wolfing down pieces of greasy mystery meat in Sierra Madre. Today's state-of-the-art burrito is slim, trim, and packed with health-conscious ingredients such as swordfish, fresh cilantro (coriander), shiitake mushrooms, raddichio, goat's cheese, arugula, cottage cheese, or fresh asparagus and more!

And you can forget the lard, too. Think canola oil, or better yet, no frying at all. Yes, you *can* enjoy mouth-watering Tex-Mex cuisine and keep your cholesterol count under control. If plain flour tortillas are terminally boring, a host of other options exist: blue corn tortillas, pita bread, rice paper, seaweed—the list goes on and on.

I hope this book will inspire you to try making this south-of-the-border sensation yourself. Virtually everyone will find something to love about burritos. Working mothers will appreciate the ease with which they can be made—often only one pan is used so clean-up is quick and easy. Budget-conscious cooks will love stuffing tortillas with lots of leftovers, then combining them with savory salsas or sauces for new taste treats. Parents of large families will enjoy the nutritious, filling meals that are easily "stretched" with beans or rice. Children will adore being encouraged to eat with their fingers! And what better way to hide those childhood horrors (lima beans, broccoli) than in a tortilla wrap? Savvy party hosts will make and freeze dozens of finger-size burritos days in advance, then serve them piping hot in 3 minutes or less at the touch of a microwave button. There's even a host of recipes for vegetarians and vegans—burrito recipes especially created for their needs that enliven the usual brown-rice-with-vegetable meal.

Burritos are well on their way to becoming as much a staple of the

American table as their distant cousin, the sandwich. Both are delicious, nutritious, offer endless variety, are easy to make, and are convenient to eat. Vivo burrito, the four-course meal you can hold in your hand!

Origin of the
Traditional Burrito

Europeans were first introduced to the burrito (little burro in Spanish) in the early 1500s, when Spanish Conquistadores, led by Cortez, invaded Mexico and encountered the Aztec civilization. Montezuma's people had as much interest in culinary art as they did in mathematics, astronomy, and engineering. The bounty of the Aztecs' terraced fields—beans, corn, sweet potatoes, avocados, tomatoes—were often rolled up in stone-ground corn tortillas that had been warmed on hot flat stones. When the Spanish introduced domesticated cattle, pigs, sheep, and goats to the Aztecs, spicy sauces and barbecued meat were added to the basic burrito. These animals also provided a more plentiful source of fats, primarily lard, which soon became the most common cooking fat used all over Mexico and Central and South America.

Chimichangas:
The Fried Burrito

While most burrito recipes utilize large wheat-flour tortillas that have been heated or steamed until pliable, the availability of lard allowed for deep-frying and the introduction of the *chimichanga* into Mexican and Southwestern cuisine. Savory fillings are rolled inside a securely folded flour tortilla, then it is plunged into sizzling fat until it turns crispy and golden brown. After a quick pat with a paper towel to remove the excess fat, the chimichanga is served garnished with guacamole or sour cream.

The Burrito Book does not offer recipes for chimichangas because I do not feel that the additional calories and increase in fat is either necessary or desirable. If you don't mind the calories and wish to create a chimichanga, simply follow the recipes included in this book, then after folding and just prior to serving, deep-fry the burrito in very hot vegetable oil (use a Fry Daddy or other deep-fat fryer rather than a skillet) for several minutes until the tortilla is light brown. Drain and serve immediately.

Enchilada-Style
Burritos

The perfect burrito is a harmonious blend of ingredients balanced with just the right amount of salsa or sauce. This book gives many recipes for guacamoles, salsas, and sauces. You can either stuff the sauce inside the tortilla with the other ingredients or cover the outside. Smothering a folded burrito with South-of-the-Border Sour Cream Sauce or Ranchera Sauce (see page 124) is another mouth-watering variation available to you. The only problem is that when you do this, you'll need a knife and fork to eat your burrito.

Of course, less sauce is necessary when portioned over ingredients layered inside a tortilla. Mint Sauce and Gila Bend Salsa Verde (see pages 129 and 126) are both better when spread sparingly on the inside of a tortilla prior to folding because of their pungent flavors. Utilizing sauce inside a burrito facilitates hands-on eating, part of the fun of making burritos in the first place. But when a rather dry burrito (such as sautéed chicken breast or stewed beef) is a bit hard to swallow, copious quantities of just the right mole or salsa make everything go down easier and taste a whole lot better.

In *The Burrito Book*, you will find burritos of both types, "all in" and smothered. Feel free to create your own recipe, then pour on one of the zesty salsas or creamy rich sauces for an entirely different treat. Chili (not chili peppers) can also be spooned over the top of burritos, and melted cheese also makes for more moistness.

Ethnic and Exotic
Burritos

While the traditional burrito as we know it began in Central Mexico at least four hundred years ago, similar types of dishes have appeared regularly worldwide. Chinese egg rolls, Greek stuffed grape leaves, Middle Eastern baklava cones, and Japanese sushi rolls are all first cousins to the Aztec burrito.

Many of the recipes I've included in this book are inspired by and based on traditional ethnic recipes that naturally lend themselves to this type of presentation. Middle Eastern and Indian dishes, in particular, are easily adaptable because they are cooked in one or two pans and are usually eaten from a single bowl. Similarly, Asian stir-fried dishes are instantly transformed when wrapped in tortillas or another type "skin" such as rice paper or softened, warm pita bread.

With a judicious eye and some practice, you will be able to turn almost any leftover into a delightfully fresh-tasting burrito feast by using an amazing variety of ingredients and wrappings. To create your own recipes, seek inspiration from local restaurants or your favorite cookbooks, then adapt the portions and preparation (particularly slicing vegetables and meat into strips or bite-size chunks) until you have a satisfying, new culinary creation.

Tortilla Tales

As we sail into the nineties, the humble handmade, rather thick and chewy tortilla is becoming a relic of the past. It seems that everywhere I go, prepackaged paper-thin tortillas (usually made with flour and lard) are the rule, even at the roadside stands throughout Mexico itself!

There are exceptions, of course; the M & J Restaurant and Sanitary Tortilla Factory in Albuquerque, New Mexico, is one of them. "Home of the Five Hongo Burrito," it defies the test of time and offers numerous sizes and styles of home-style tortillas as well as delicious Mexican fare underneath its Spanish tile roof.

To rectify this, I've included a recipe for Homemade Corn Tortillas on page 8, and I heartily encourage you to scour your phone book for local Mexican specialty shops and tortillarias.

Of course, grocery stores now offer an amazing variety of tortillas, too: blue corn, whole wheat, flour (with or without lard), and corn come in diameters ranging from 4 inches (for hand-held soft tacos) to 18 inches (for tostado-shell frying). Most cooks will appreciate the convenience of this; however, once you've sampled a homemade, still hot, hand-patted tortilla, you may never go back to machine-rolled again!

Recipes in this book call for many varieties of tortillas, but presume portions fitted to the standard 8-inch tortilla. Should you not be able to obtain the proper type tortilla, simply substitute what is available. Burritos vary in size and shape from cook to cook, so there is no sole "right way" to roll one up. "How to Warm and Fold a Burrito" (see page 22) and "How to Eat a Burrito" (see page 147) will give you basic guidelines and helpful suggestions.

However, tortillas need not always be used for these recipes. Crêpes, flat breads such as split pitas, rice paper (commonly known as egg-roll wrapping), grape leaves, and other foldable edibles are also possibilities. While these recipes call for tortillas only, do not be afraid to try something new. Crêpes make delicious dessert burritos. Try layers of rice paper to make fried chimichanga-style burritos.

Homemade Corn Tortillas

There are many varieties and sizes of tortilla. The most common, large flour and small corn, are stocked in virtually every supermarket across the United States. More exotic varieties, such as whole wheat and blue corn, are carried in some supermarkets and specialty grocery stores. For those who insist on the ultimate in freshness, this recipe yields a dozen medium-size tortillas that are slightly thicker than the store-bought variety. They are more suitable for jelly roll folding than either classic or pocket square folds. The hint here is to roll each dough ball as thinly as possible.

1¼ cups white flour	2 Tb. vegetable oil
¾ cup yellow cornmeal	1 cup water
¾ tsp. salt	Oil (or PAM corn oil spray)

Combine flour, cornmeal, and salt; set aside. Add vegetable oil to water and boil in medium saucepan. Remove from heat; add dry ingredients and mix well. Cool.

Divide cooled dough into 12 balls. Roll each ball into a very thin, flat disk (think crêpes!) between two sheets of wax paper. Lightly oil a skillet (or use a light spray of corn oil PAM) and warm over medium heat for 1 minute. Place a tortilla in skillet, making sure all edges are flat; lightly brown, turning frequently. Remove and place on board to cool. Repeat cooking process until all tortillas are cooked.

Yield: 12 tortillas

NOTE: Some brown spots may appear during cooking, this is normal; however, black spots mean that the heat must be lowered. Tortillas can be prepared ahead of time and frozen by placing sheets of wax paper between each disk and stacking them inside a freezer bag. To reheat, warm tortillas individually in a lightly oiled skillet, or steam them.

If tortillas rip during filling process, they have been rolled too thin. If it is difficult to fold tortillas, they have been rolled too thick. If tortillas stick to rolling pin, you have forgotten to place wax paper on top of, as well as below, dough ball. If tortillas turn black around the edge and bubble in the middle, you've put too much oil in the skillet. You should barely coat skillet bottom with oil or cooking spray.

VARIATIONS: Tortillas can be flavored with a variety of spices. Try adding 1 teaspoon chili powder, or 2 teaspoons dill to the dough mass before separating. For dessert burritos, you may wish to add 1 teaspoon each sugar and cinnamon to the dough mixture.

Do not give up hope if your first efforts fail. Tortilla making is considered an art all over Mexico, as well as Central and South America. It often takes the daughter of the house years of daily practice before she can assume the responsibilities of the tortilleñas. Experiment by making slight adjustments to the recipe (opposite) to find out the particular dough consistency that works best for you.

Beans, Lentils, and Peas

Beans, lentils, and peas are available dried, canned, or frozen in hundreds of taste-tempting varieties and are an excellent choice for filling a burrito. Look beyond the traditional pinto bean and you will find an endless assortment suitable for stretching meager amounts of meat or fowl, as well as adding desirable substance to vegetarian recipes.

Listed on the following pages are descriptions and simple cooking instructions for fifteen commonly available legumes that will enliven your basic burrito. Smart cooks know that even the most finicky child will accept lima beans or lentils, as long as they are hidden inside a tortilla and combined with other favorite foods.

ADZUKI BEANS have a mildly sweet flavor and a soft texture. Their appealing brown skin is often split with lovely white fracture patterns. At my house, we call adzuki "Indian paint horse beans" because of the similarity in color and design. Soak the beans in cold water overnight; drain, then boil for 10 minutes in three parts water to one part beans. Lower heat and cover pot, then simmer for 2 hours.

BLACK BEANS, a.k.a. *frijoles negroes*, are very common beans in the Southwest and Mexico that are finding acceptance nationally. I like them because they can be cooked from scratch without lard and still retain a full, earthy flavor. Their rather mealy texture is interesting, and these beans are easily mashed or pureed for an alternative to refried beans. Soak beans in cold water overnight; drain, then boil for 10 minutes in three parts water to one part beans. Lower heat and cover pot, then simmer for 1 hour.

BLACK-EYED PEAS are extremely popular in Texas and most of the South, but they also make for a wonderful addition to either meat or fowl burrito recipes. Their earthy flavor and slightly firm, succulent texture help them fill out an otherwise skimpy array of vegetables and meat. When cooked with onion, they are delectable. Soak peas in cold water overnight; drain, then boil in three parts water to one part beans for 3 minutes. Lower heat and cover pot, then simmer for 1 hour.

FAVA BEANS are exceptionally large, meaty beans with a strong (almost bitter) flavor and granular texture. They are also sold under the name broad beans in some parts of the States. Fava beans are common in Middle Eastern cooking and are usually combined with ripe red tomatoes and spices to sweeten their temperament. Because of their substantial size, they are a good substitute for meat in burritos, especially when combined with an equal portion of rice or grain. Soak beans in cold water overnight; drain, then peel off the bitter brown skins before cooking. Boil cleaned beans for 10 minutes in three parts water to one part beans; lower heat, cover pot, and simmer for 2 hours.

GARBANZO BEANS, or chick-peas, are another centuries-old staple for which recipes can be found throughout the Middle East and Mediterranean. In more recent times, they have become a popular addition in many forms throughout the Southwest and Mexico. With their delectably nutty flavor and unusual texture (mealy when cooked, almost crunchy when raw), they are a versatile favorite for both burritos and side dishes. Soak in cold water overnight; drain, and boil in three parts water to one part beans for 3 minutes. Lower heat, cover pot, and simmer for 2 hours.

GREAT NORTHERN BEANS are cream colored with a mild flavor and mealy texture. If cooked too long they will become mushy, so when adding them to burritos make sure to drain all excess liquid well. These beans readily absorb the flavor of spices or other ingredients and are an excellent choice if a recipe needs to be "stretched." Soak beans in cold water overnight; drain, and boil for 10 minutes in three parts water to one part beans. Lower heat, cover pot, and simmer for 2 hours.

GREEN PEAS are actually common field peas and are sometimes yellow or yellowish green in color. They have a sweet taste and soft texture when cooked, and are easily added to either meat or fowl burrito recipes that are not heavily spiced. I've found that chili powder is at complete odds with the delicate flavor of peas and do not often combine the two in the same recipe. The split pea is not very useful in burrito recipes as it tends to get extremely mushy during the cooking process; it should be used for soups. Soak peas in cold water overnight; drain, and bring to a boil in three parts water to one part peas. Lower heat, cover pot, and simmer for 1 hour.

KIDNEY BEANS are one of my favorites for making burritos and chili. Their firm/mealy texture and hearty taste are the perfect complement to ground beef or strips of steak or lamb. Available in either red or white varieties, kidney beans do not squash easily and so are a recommended choice for all-in-one-pan-style burrito preparation. Soak in cold water overnight; drain, and boil for 10 minutes in three parts water to one part beans. Lower heat, cover pot, and simmer for 1½ hours.

LENTILS come in dozens of varieties worldwide and have been a staple food of the human family for centuries. Commonly available in green (pungent flavor) or red (really a medium brown color with bland flavor) varieties, lentils have a soft, yielding texture when cooked properly. Most novice cooks do not soak lentils long enough, and they tend to serve them slightly underdone. Lentils, green or red, are quite hardy and can take much abuse in terms of improper preparation, but with a little care in the kitchen they can become the basis for building many types of burritos. Bring to a boil in three parts water to one part whole lentils; lower heat, cover pot, and simmer for 20 minutes. Do not let lentils overcook or they will turn to mush.

LIMA BEANS (and broccoli) are the bane of many childhoods, but these medium-size chartreuse-colored beans are an excellent choice for burrito filling. Lima beans have a medium to soft texture (try not to overcook, or the skins will blister off and the beans will turn to mush) and a rather bland flavor. They readily absorb flavor from freshly crushed garlic or onion powder and cooked tomatoes (simmer for best flavor absorption). Soak in cold water overnight; drain, and boil for 10 minutes in three parts water to one part beans. Lower heat, cover pot, and simmer for 1½ hours.

MUNG BEANS are odd-looking tiny dark green, brown, or black beans with a soft texture and slightly sweet flavor similar to green peas. Packed with nutrients, mung beans are an acceptable substitute for peas in many burrito recipes. Soak in cold water for three hours; drain, and bring to a boil in three parts water to one part beans. Lower heat, cover pot, and simmer for 30 minutes.

NAVY BEANS are another very common variety that easily take on whatever seasoning or dominant food flavor they are paired with. Their whitish color, mild flavor, and mealy texture make them a good choice for portion stretching since they do not distort the original taste balance of the burrito's ingredients. Soak beans in cold water overnight; drain, and boil for 10 minutes in three parts water to one part beans. Lower heat, cover pot, and simmer for 1½ hours.

PINTO BEANS are the staple legume of Mexico, Central America, and much of the southwestern United States. They can be boiled, baked, or fried (commonly known as refried beans). Their cheerfully mottled brown and cream appearance disappears when they are cooked, turning into a consistent light brown. Very earthy in flavor, they are usually prepared with animal fat for additional taste. Their mealy texture is palatable either boiled whole, or when mashed or pureed (see Basic Refried Beans on page 14). Soak in cold water overnight; drain, boil for 10 minutes in three parts water to one part beans. Lower heat, cover pot, and simmer for 1½ hours. Do not overcook or beans will turn to mush.

RED BEANS are the famous traditional Louisiana poor-boy supper of Red Beans and Rice; however, red beans are also a good choice for burritos. Their mildy sweet flavor and mealy texture make them the perfect choice for fowl or pork, they are commonly found canned on supermarket shelves, and they readily accept seasoning, particularly chili powder. Soak in cold water overnight; drain, then boil for 10 minutes in three parts water to one part beans. Lower heat, cover pot, and simmer for 2 hours.

SOYBEANS are an extremely nutritious legume; they have become a staple in the diet of virtually all Asian countries, as well as a favorite with health-food fans here in America. Soybeans are extremely versatile and many disparate products have been created using these firmly textured, mildly flavored beans; some products include soy milk, tempeh (a chickenlike meat substitute), frozen desserts, and noodles. They come in many varieties including yellow, green, brown, black, or mottled. Soak in cold water overnight; drain, and boil for 10 minutes in three parts water to one part beans. Lower heat, cover pot, and simmer for 1½ hours.

Basic Refried Beans

▼ ▼ ▼

1 lb. dried pinto beans	1 clove garlic, minced
1 cup diced onions	½ cup tomato paste
½ cup lard*	2 tsp. chili powder

Wash beans well and place in large saucepan with onions; just cover with water. Cover, then bring water to a rolling boil. Reduce heat and simmer until beans are tender, 2½–3 hours. Check hourly to see if more water is needed; if so, add in ¼ cup amounts so that water continues to boil.

Drain water and mash beans with ¼ cup lard. Heat remaining lard in separate skillet; when melted, add garlic and gently brown. Add mashed beans and continue cooking until all lard is absorbed by beans, stirring constantly to prevent sticking. Add tomato paste and chili powder, stir thoroughly, and serve as is or utilize in burrito filling.

Yield: 3 cups

*Lard can be replaced by an equal amount of bacon drippings for more flavor, or by vegetable shortening (for very bland beans).

Rice and Grain

While Spanish Rice (see page 18) is a commonly accepted side dish for many Mexican or Southwestern-style meals, there is also a wealth of other grains and rices that are perfectly suitable as burrito fillings.

I encourage you to experiment with mixing grains together to create unique texture contrasts and flavor undertones; cooking instructions and descriptions of some appropriate rices and grains are listed on the following pages.

BARLEY GROATS are medium-brown-colored, unpolished whole kernels with a mild flavor and chewy texture that complements pork, lamb, or beef exceptionally well. Bring groats to boil in two parts water to one part groats; lower heat, cover pot, and simmer for 1 hour.

BARLEY PEARLS are tiny white whole kernels that have been frequently polished; polishing removes the husk, bran, and germ of each single kernel. Polished grains cook much faster than unpolished ones, and the process often changes the texture and flavor as well as the appearance of the kernel. Barley pearls (also known as soup barley) are suitable for almost any type of burrito filling as they have a tender texture and very mild taste. Bring barley to boil in one part water to two parts barley; lower heat, cover pot, and simmer for 30 minutes.

BROWN RICE has long been known as a vegetarian staple food, but these unpolished grains with their firm texture and nutlike flavor are steadily growing in popularity in all parts of the United States. The nutritional value of brown rice over white has long been touted by medical doctors, but I prefer using brown rice because it tastes so good. It also comes in long-, medium-, or short-grain varieties. Bring rice to a boil in two parts water to one part rice; lower heat, cover pot, and simmer for 45 minutes.

BUCKWHEAT GROATS have a decidedly nutlike flavor and a rather soft texture. These whole, unpolished kernels should be used sparingly (no more than ¼ cup per burrito), or mixed with another grain or beans to temper their flavor. Buckwheat groats, when toasted, are called kasha. Bring groats to a boil in two parts water to one part groats; lower heat, cover pot, and simmer for 15 minutes.

CRACKED HOMINY are dried, split kernels of either yellow or white corn, soaked to remove the bran. When cooked they have a firm texture and are mildly sweet. I use them with fowl or fish burritos but prefer using fresh or canned hominy overall. Soak hominy in cold water overnight; drain. Bring hominy to a boil in three parts water to one part hominy; lower heat, cover pot, and simmer for 2½ hours. Check doneness and continue cooking for 15–20 minutes more if necessary.

GLUTINOUS RICE is an Asian favorite, but I find these extremely sticky grains suitable for several recipes. This rice has a sweet flavor and makes a wonderful base for Payson Pudding (see recipe page 143) or as a filler for fruit-filled dessert burritos. Glutinous rice is polished whole kernels of a very short-grain variety (some grains look almost round). Soak rice in cold water overnight; drain. Bring rice to boil in one part water to one part rice; lower heat, cover pot, and simmer for 10 minutes.

OAT GROATS are another unpolished whole kernel with a light brown color, chewy texture, and sweet, almost nutty, flavor. Thinner and slightly more pliable than barley groats, this grain is suitable for some fowl dishes (particularly turkey) as well as pork, beef, or lamb. Bring groats to boil in two parts water to one part groats; lower heat, cover pot, and simmer for 1 hour.

WHEAT BERRIES are whole, unpolished kernels with a toasty color and very chewy texture when cooked. Their strong, rather earthy flavor complements almost any eggplant-and-stewed-tomato-based burrito recipe, or adds taste to mild fowl such as chicken. Wheat berries are rapidly gaining popularity outside of health-food circles as we move into the health conscious nineties. When the kernels are steamed, dried, then cracked, they are called bulgur. The processing softens the wheat berries' texture without sacrificing much flavor. However, bulgur tends to turn into mush if not carefully cooked, so it is usually deemed unsuitable for burrito fillings. Bring wheat berries to boil in two parts water to one part wheat berries; lower heat, cover pot, and simmer for 1 hour.

WHITE RICE is highly polished, firmly textured with virtually no flavor of its own. It comes in long, medium, or short grains and readily absorbs any seasoning or flavoring (such as chicken broth or spiced tomato sauce) readily, making it a favorite of cooks all over the United States. Bring rice to boil in 1¾ parts water to 1 part rice; lower heat, cover pot, and simmer for 12 minutes. If you prefer softer rice, continue cooking for 2–3 more minutes.

WILD RICE is elegant black or deep chocolate brown kernels that are extremely slender and chewy when cooked. Because of its very strong nutlike flavor, wild rice is most often mixed with brown and white rice kernels rather than served on its own. These whole unpolished kernels are perfect with all manner of fowl. Bring rice to boil in three parts water to one part rice; lower heat, cover pot, and simmer for 1 hour.

Basic Spanish Rice

Rice has been served with most Mexican dishes for centuries. It can be served in large bowls alongside entrées or used as part of a burrito stuffing. When mixed with an equal portion of beans, complete proteins are formed that are necessary to the health of vegetarians or those on a severely restricted budget. Many varieties of rice exist, but most recipes for Spanish rice call for either long-grain white or brown rice. Those watching their cholesterol count may wish to eliminate the bacon and sauté the green pepper in canola oil or wine instead. This particular recipe comes from a little restaurant across from the Jai Alai palace in Tijuana, Mexico; when I asked the proprietress where the recipe had come from, she smiled and said "*Nada*" (roughly translated, "From nowhere" or, more likely, "Who knows?").

4 medium tomatoes, quartered	5 drops Tabasco sauce
2¼ cups water	1 tsp. molasses
1 small onion, chopped	1 cup chopped tomatoes
1 cup brown rice	½ cup chopped fresh parsley
2 chicken bouillon cubes	½ cup canned tomato sauce
2 tsp. garlic paste	6 slices bacon
1 tsp. seasoned salt	½ large green pepper, diced

Place quartered tomatoes and water in blender jar; puree. Pour into large pot, add onion, and boil. Add rice, bouillon cubes, garlic paste, salt, Tabasco, and molasses. Lower heat and simmer, covered, until rice has absorbed almost all the water (usually 40–45 minutes). Add chopped tomatoes, parsley, and tomato sauce, stir well, and cover. Fry bacon crisp in skillet; remove and blot on paper towels. Sauté green pepper in bacon drippings; remove using slotted spoon and add to rice mixture. Crumble bacon and add to rice mixture. Mix well and remove from heat.

Preheat oven to 350 degrees.

Lightly oil bottom of 1-quart casserole; pour rice mixture into it and bake for 20 minutes, or until rice is tender.

Yield: 3 cups

Chilies

The word *chili* has been traced back to the Aztecs of Central Mexico and describes many types of hot peppers used in cooking. Before we get into the many varieties of chilies available fresh, canned, or dried, I have a word of caution—HOT! The flesh of a chili is not as hot as the seeds and ribs, which contain enough incendiary power to fly a rocket during the right season of the year. Some handling precautions are therefore recommended as follows.

Handle raw chilies using rubber gloves. Touching the skin, seeds, or ribs of a powerful pepper can be painful or even dangerous if your bare fingers touch your mouth or eyes. Make sure to work next to a sink so you can flush a stinging lip or eye with cool water. Some people even find the pungent aroma of numerous peppers somewhat irritating (think of crying when cutting onions); try opening a window or switching on a fan to disperse the spicy aromatic scent.

If your chilies are too spicy, remove the seeds and ribs before using in a burrito or other recipe. Also try experimenting with different chilies for different tastes and levels of heat. There are more than 65 varieties of chili in Mexico and the United States, and many listed below are commonly found in your neighborhood supermarket.

Some recipes in this book feature raw chilies, while others specify canned. The latter are almost always preroasted (such as Anaheim, or long green chilies), or treated in some way (pickled jalapeños).

If you would like to dry your own chilies for future use, simply use a needle and thread to string the caps of fully ripened peppers together, then hang them from the ceiling for at least a week in warm, dry weather. Immature chilies will rot; humidity can often cause mold to form on the peppers. Chilies can also be spread on a screen and left out in the sun on hot summer days (just make sure that animals, birds, or children do not have access to them). Once the chilies are dried, they can be crushed into powder and stored in a spice jar, or placed in a plastic freezer bag and frozen for future use. I do not recommend leaving dried chilies hanging as they will invite all manner of bugs and spiders, as well as grow dusty prior to use.

Roasting your own chilies is easy; simply place them on a broiler rack and grill them until the top side is toasty brown (not black or burned), flip the pepper over, and repeat the process. The chilies' skins will bubble and possibly split; remove the skin by peeling under cool water.

ANAHEIM is a mild chili that grows from 6—8 inches in length and is usually a glossy green, though sometimes they are allowed to vine ripen until partly or totally orange-red. They are commonly stuffed in the Tex-Mex dish of Chile Relleno, but are also used extensively in burritos. Normally one whole Anaheim chili will be enough for one burrito when additional fillings are added, such as shredded chicken, melted cheddar, and sliced olives. Many companies offer these chilies whole or diced in small cans already preroasted and ready to use. Flavor, not heat, is provided by these chilies.

ARBOL is a skinny little thing (only 2—3 inches long) but it packs an amazingly hot wallop. Heat, not flavor, is the key here. Arbols are usually sold as mature red-colored peppers, but can also be mottled green and red or solid green.

CHERRY PEPPERS are fairly round red or green peppers (depending on maturity) a little smaller than a golf ball. They are spicy, but not exceptionally hot, and usually found pickled with cauliflower and carrots in Mexican relishes.

CHIPOTLE chilies are rarely sold fresh but are extremely common canned. They are actually smoked, slightly charred jalapeño peppers and retain much of that famous fiery jalapeño heat through the cooking process. Many Southwestern and Tex-Mex recipes call for dried chipotle peppers; you will recognize them by their medium brown color and rough-skinned texture. A good chipotle sauce is cause for recognition in some rural areas of Mexico and usually smothers boiled chicken.

HABANERO peppers are commonly used in making salsa in the Yucatan part of Mexico. Their golden-orange color denotes their fiery disposition; the seeds alone are almost hot enough to self-combust! One 2-inch-long pepper (rather puffy and bloated looking) is powerful enough to flavor an entire bowl of tomato salsa.

HUNGARIAN WAX chilies are usually sold fresh when no bigger than 3 inches long and a mild yellow color. Try to let them ripen a bit (more canary yellow) at room temperature before cooking, or look for peppers with orange spots on them. Their distinctive flavor and medium-hot heat make them perfect for stir-frying or using raw in three-pepper-style salsas.

JALAPEÑO is the most infamous of chilies north of the border. It is approximately 2 inches long, and deep green to green with red splotches. While the power of their heat varies from season to season, it's a safe bet to consider these little gems incendiary all year round. A little goes a long way, and the removal of seeds is almost a necessity unless you're willing to melt your tastebuds. Jalapeños can be used in salsas or as burrito fillings, side dish flavorings, relishes, and more.

NEGRO chili is the commonly found dried version of the pasilla pepper, which is commonly confused and marketed as a poblano in parts of Baja and Southern California. The pasilla is a darker green, slightly slimmer and has a blunter end; it usually grows between 4 and 5 inches in length. After being roasted, it is used in Mexican entrées such as tamales and quesadillas. When dried, it is the basis for a very rich, dark, thick sauce that has much flavor without a lot of heat. Raw or dried, the pasilla is mild to medium hot.

POBLANO (known as ancho or mulato when dried) is puffier and slightly longer than a pasilla pepper and has a much sharper tip. It is extremely common in both raw and dried forms, and is used extensively in many popular Mexican recipes including rellenos, tamales, sauces, and salsas. It is mild to medium hot with a warm, delicious flavor.

SERRANO is a small green pepper 1½–2 inches long. It is very skinny and often confused with the jalapeño; look for shine when comparing the two, as the jalapeño has more sheen. Serranos can be used the same way jalapeños are, for virtually everything that requires a very hot pepper. For less heat, remove seeds and all ribs.

How to Warm
and Fold a Burrito

The secrets to successfully folding a burrito are simple:

1. Always warm the tortilla first
2. Match the folding style to the ingredients
3. Make sure the bottom doesn't fall out

Warming the Tortilla

While restaurants usually utilize an expensive steamer specifically designed to speedily moisten and warm the fresh or prepackaged tortillas, most at-home chefs must come up with creative alternatives. Simply placing them on a cookie sheet and sticking them in a hot oven will not work; tortillas dry out and become brittle very quickly.

The most successful way to heat tortillas without having them dry out is to microwave them 30—60 seconds. Alternately layer tortillas and moistened paper towels on a microwave-safe plate, making sure that the tortillas lay flat and that you stack no more than a dozen tortillas in this manner, ending with a damp paper towel on top.

Since microwaves differ in heating capability, experiment with cooking times and rotation. The tortillas should come out warm, pliable, and fragrant. If they come out dry or crisp, use more water on the paper towels. If they come out soggy, use less water and stack fewer layers.

If you do not have a microwave, you may try this method in a preheated 250-degree or less oven; watch carefully to make sure the tortillas remain pliable. If they have become brittle, do what I do: throw them in some hot oil and fry them for chips! Then try again, making sure the paper towels are well saturated and the tortillas are not left in the oven overlong.

Another method uses a large, inexpensive vegetable steamer, available at most grocery, department, and discount stores. This item is also known as a ''broccoli steamer'' in some areas. Loosely roll (do not fold) the tortillas and place inside the device, then steam over boiling water for 60 seconds. You can only steam two to four tortillas at a time this way, so plan ahead.

A favorite way of mine to steam tortillas was discovered on a car-camping trip in the impossibly hot Baja desert. After many long, bone-jarring miles of driving on a rabbit path that the government optimistically called the "free road," we stopped at a tiny, ramshackle shed that promised "comida de la mer." While there were a couple of battered lobsters simmering in an evil-looking pot, it was the cook's use of a huge cast-iron skillet that could not go unnoticed.

At first the cook dropped in six thick slices of fatty bacon, crisping them in record time and scooping them out to "drain" on the napkin-covered wood counter. Then, in a series of magnificent contortions (there was barely enough room to change your mind in this shed) and with perfect timing, he added raw eggs, a handful of shredded chicken meat, some mysterious looking greens, and some chili salsa. As these began to sizzle, he covered the pan with a square of bug netting (yes, window screen) and plopped four tortillas on top. After a minute, he removed the tortillas and expertly filled them with the skillet mess.

Needless to say, the potentially hazardous ingredients tasted delicious and the tortillas were perfect: not too dry, not too soggy. They did not rip, tear, or shred, and held the filling admirably. If the idea of bug netting turns you off, I'd suggest using a splash guard (those large, round metal contraptions with screen that look a bit like tennis rackets and are used to keep fried foods from splashing during the cooking process).

Simply pour a cup or so of water into your largest skillet, place the splash guard on top of the pan's rim, and turn the heat on high. Once you have a rolling boil, place the tortillas flat on the guard and steam individually 30–60 seconds. For extra-thick tortillas, you may wish to turn the tortilla over and steam each side 45–60 seconds.

The Jelly-Roll Fold

This is the easiest fold to master, but the least usable as most chunky fillings would fall out of the bottom if the burrito is hand held. However, this enchilada-style fold is excellent for pan-baked burritos designed for knife-and-fork consumption. (See pages 24–25.)

Place the warm tortilla on a board or plate. Spread filling evenly on the top side, making sure to leave a ½-inch border around the edge. Starting at one end, roll up like a jelly roll (or a carpet) and continue to roll until entire tortilla has a log shape. Serve seam-side down (or place in baking dish seam-side down, cover in sauce, bake, and serve using a spatula).

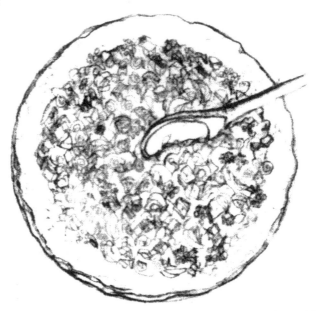

Step 1. Spread filling evenly over surface of tortilla, leaving ½" border all the way around.

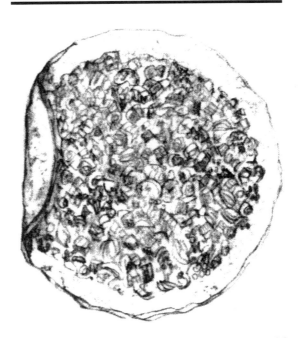

Step 2. Starting at one end, roll up like a carpet, tucking under left edge.

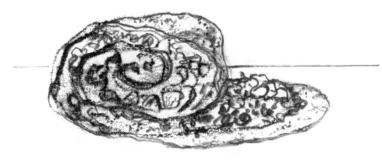

Step 3. (Sideview) Continue rolling until entire filled tortilla has a log shape.

Step 4. Serve seam-side down and drizzle with sauce.

The Classic Fold

This is the traditional shape for a burrito with smooth to semichunky fillings, fillings that utilize either a gravy or sauce, or a filling that may become runny when heated (some cheeses). The folded edges ensure that there is no spillage from the bottom if the burrito is hand held. (See below and opposite.)

Place warmed tortilla flat on a board or plate. Spread filling on top, leaving a ¾–1-inch border around the edge. Fold over right and left sides of tortilla until outer edges meet in the middle; press slightly to hold in place. Starting at bottom of tortilla, roll up like a carpet, making sure the folded sides are fixed firmly in the roll. If a side fold becomes unstuck, simply unroll the burrito and begin again. Serve seam-side down.

Classic Fold

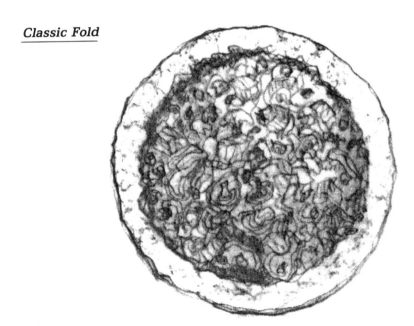

Step 1. Spread filling evenly over surface of tortilla, leaving ¾"–1" border all the way around.

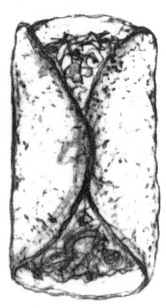

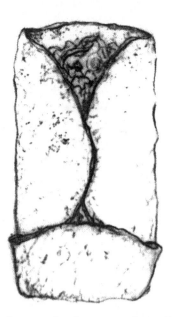

Step 2. Fold over right and left sides of tortilla until outer edges meet in the middle.

Step 3. Starting at the bottom of tortilla, roll up like a carpet, making sure the folded sides are fixed firmly in the roll.

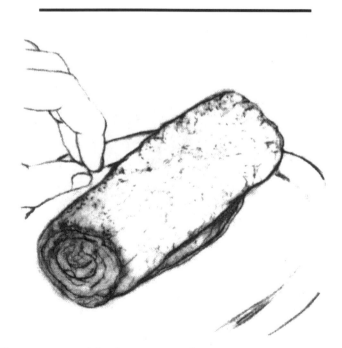

Step 4. Serve seam-side down, eat with hands or knife and fork.

The Pocket-Square Fold

Especially good for very chunky fillings (such as authentic chili with cubes of meat and onion) or recipes where the burrito is to be fried. Shorter and more squat than the classic fold, the pocket square is also easier to hold in the hand and is more sturdy than other styles. (See below and opposite.)

Place the heated tortilla on a board or plate. Spoon filling (or use large ice cream scoop) on center of tortilla. Fold top of tortilla over half of the filling. Fold the left side over slightly more than half the filling; then fold the right side, slightly overlapping the left-hand fold. Finally, fold the bottom up and over both sides so that the bottom edge rests in the center of a neat square. Using the palm of your hand, press the pocket square *gently* so that the burrito is fairly flat on top (rather than bulging). Serve seam-side down.

Pocket-Square Fold

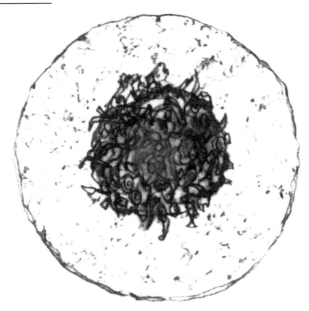

Step 1. Spoon filling, using spoon or ice cream scooper, onto center of tortilla.

Step 2. Fold top down over half the filling.

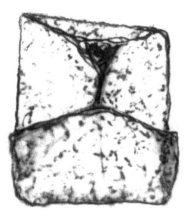

Step 3. Fold left side over slightly more than half the filling; then fold right side, overlapping left-hand fold. Fold bottom up over both sides, so bottom edge rests in center of a neat square.

Step 4. Using the palm of your hand, press burrito *gently* so that the surface is fairly flat on top. Serve seam-side down; eat with hands or knife and fork.

A Word to the Wise

Do not roll burritos too tight or some filling ingredients (such as zucchini spears or asparagus) may push through the tortilla creating a tear. Do not overfill burritos; it is better to make many smaller burritos than have the bottom of a massive burrito collapse because of the weight of too many ingredients. Spread or spoon filling evenly; burritos should not have lumps or be shaped like pears (bottom heavy).

If you are using a recipe with gravy, you may decide to use two tortillas per burrito instead of one; simply lay one heated tortilla on top of the other and fold as usual. Likewise, if you are deep-frying, you may opt to use a second tortilla to thicken the burrito skin and keep ingredients from bubbling out during the cooking process.

If you rip a burrito after you've folded it, do not despair. Simply unfold the burrito and place it (ripped tortilla and all) on top of a second warmed tortilla. Since tortillas are very thin, the second skin will hide the rip without adding undesirable bulk.

Tortilla Alternatives

If you tire of using tortillas, you can replace them in certain recipes with their high-class cousins—crêpes—or with rice paper (more commonly known as Chinese egg roll skins). Certain Middle Eastern and European flat breads also lend themselves to the jelly-roll fold and can be used. Flat rounds of pita bread, split carefully in half along the seams rather than cut lengthwise as usual, can be heated in the same way as a tortilla and rolled or folded.

STARTERS

▼ ▼ ▼

Before you sit down to grapple with the burrito of your choice, you may want a couple of dishes or drinks to warm up for the entrée. The following are a few of the many alternatives to chips, dips, and cocktails that I've found.

Beverages

Loco Leche

▼ ▼ ▼

A wild drink for adults only, this is a sweetly intoxicating punch that's a perfect accompaniment for dessert burritos. Versions I've heard about include those made with tequila, rum and tequila, and even one from a tipsy Mexicali tourist that featured chocolate milk! Ugh! This is very tame by comparison.

▲ ▲ ▲

2 Tb. cornstarch	5 eggs, lightly beaten
5 cups whole milk	3¼ cups rum
¾ cup sugar	½ tsp. vanilla extract
5 tsp. ground cinnamon	

Mix the cornstarch with 2 Tb. of the milk in a large bowl and set aside. Scald remaining milk over medium heat in a large saucepan; pour hot milk into cornstarch-milk mixture, stirring constantly until blended. Pour contents of bowl back into pan and place pan back on medium heat; bring mixture to a boil, stirring constantly. Reduce heat to low and simmer for 2 minutes, stirring constantly. Remove pan from heat; add sugar, cinnamon, and eggs, blending well (there should be no little lumps). Pour contents of pan back into bowl and stir in rum and vanilla. Cover bowl and chill for at least 1 hour. Stir once before pouring into serving glasses.

Yield: 8 cups, or 16 ½-cup servings (serves 8)

Sangria

▼ ▼ ▼

This fruity wine punch from Spain is an excellent beverage for most burritos. While purists will shudder at the notion of drinking red wine with poultry or fish, it is commonly done in the warmer climes.

▲ ▲ ▲

6 **cups red wine**	**Ice cubes**
1 **cup water**	1 **lemon, thinly sliced**
⅓ **cup sugar**	1 **orange, thinly sliced**
¼ **cup fresh lemon juice**	

In a large pitcher or punch bowl, combine wine and water. In small mixing bowl, combine sugar and lemon juice, stirring until sugar crystals have dissolved; add mixture to wine and stir well. Add ice cubes and lemon and orange slices; stir well and serve.

Yield: 8 cups (serves 4–8)

Classic Strawberry Margarita

▼ ▼ ▼

¼ oz. fresh lemon or lime juice

¼ oz. Cointreau

1½ oz. tequila

1 scoop crushed ice

7 fresh ripe strawberries

Mix ingredients, except for 1 strawberry, in a blender until smooth and frosty. Pour into iced cocktail glass and garnish with 1 strawberry.

Yield: 1 serving

Melon Margarita

▼ ▼ ▼

1 Tb. lime juice

¼ oz. Midori

1½ oz. tequila

½ cup 1-inch cubes cantaloupe

1 scoop crushed ice

1 wafer-thin slice lime

Mix first five ingredients in blender until smooth and frosty. Pour into iced cocktail glass and garnish with lime slice.

Yield: 1 serving

Classic Margarita

▼ ▼ ▼

1 tsp. sugar

¼ oz. lemon juice

¼ oz. sweet-and-sour mix

1½ oz. tequila

1 scoop crushed ice

Whipped cream

Mint sprig

Mix first five ingredients in blender until smooth and frosty. Pour into iced cocktail glass and garnish with dollop of whipped cream and mint sprig.

Yield: 1 serving

Soups

Rosarita Beach Clam Soup

▼ ▼ ▼

On one of her many trips into Baja, California, my friend Barbara Klein (co-owner and executive chef of Serrano's restaurant in Sedona, Arizona) stopped at a small Pacific coastal village called Rosarita Beach. The local hotel is an incredibly popular "watering hole" for Norte Americanos, but Barbara and her traveling companion decided instead to wander through the dusty streets in search of a little adventure. She discovered some beautiful fresh clams for sale and purchased them immediately. In her motorhome, Barbara improvised and whipped up this lively seaside soup. "At home," she explains, "I use canned clams and it turns out fine."

▲ ▲ ▲

10 oz. bottled clam juice

Two 4½-oz. cans minced clams with juice

3 cups water

One 28-oz. can whole peeled tomatoes, diced, juice reserved

1 small onion, chopped

4 carrots, sliced

1 cup chopped celery leaves

6 unpeeled red potatoes, chopped

¼ tsp. fennel seed

1 garlic clove, minced

⅛ tsp. white pepper

⅓ cup tomato sauce

Combine all ingredients in large soup pot and cook for 1 hour.
   Yield: Serves 8

Mexico City Winter Soup

▼ ▼ ▼

Yes, Virginia, winter does come to this sun-drenched city, and it is at plaza-side cafés that visitors and locals alike indulge in this hearty soup. While often served in small bowls as a warming prelude to some sizzling, spicy-hot entrée, it can also be dished up in big earthenware crocks alongside a loaf of freshly baked brown bread and vats of butter for a meal in itself.

▲ ▲ ▲

One 5-lb. stewing hen

1 large onion, cut into chunks

1 carrot, sliced into ¼-inch disks

2 tsp. salt

1 tsp. chili powder

1 tsp. black pepper

3 quarts water

1 green bell pepper, seeded and sliced into rings

6 oz. can garbanzo beans, drained and rinsed

6 oz. can kidney beans, drained and rinsed

6 oz. can corn, drained and rinsed

8 oz. jalapeño jack cheese, cut into ½-inch cubes

1 ripe avocado, peeled, pit removed, thinly sliced, and sprinkled with lemon juice

Put chicken in a large pot with onion, carrot, salt, chili powder, and pepper. Pour water over chicken (add more water, if necessary, so that chicken is covered completely). Turn heat to high and bring water to a boil; lower heat to medium-low and simmer chicken for 2 hours, or until tender.

Remove chicken from pot and wrap in aluminum foil to keep it warm. Raise heat to high and boil the stock for 15 minutes, then reduce heat to medium-high, skimming off any excess fat that rises to the surface. Add the bell pepper and turn heat to medium-low, simmering for 10 minutes; add garbanzos, kidney beans, and corn, and continue simmering for 5 more minutes. While soup is simmering, uncover the chicken and remove meat from bones; return chicken to pot. Keep simmering until chicken is thoroughly heated.

Using large ladle, spoon soup into deep bowls; divide cheese and avocado slices among the bowls and serve immediately.

Yield: Serves 6–8 for main course; serves 12 for first course

Yucatan Lime Chicken Soup

One of my favorite recipes by Barbara Klein (co-owner and executive chef of Serrano's restaurant in Sedona, Arizona), this soup's slightly tangy undertone really tantalizes tastebuds and is a wonderful first or second course for family meals. If you choose not to fry your own corn tortillas, you can crumble 12 lightly salted (or no-salt) tortilla chips into bowls instead.

8 cups chicken stock

1 small onion, minced

7 oz. can diced green chilies

One 28-oz. can whole peeled tomatoes, chopped (plus can juice!)

2 cloves garlic, minced

2 cups cooked, shredded chicken

¼ tsp. ground cumin

⅛ tsp. white pepper

1 lime, quartered

2 corn tortillas, cut into ½-in. strips, fried crisp

1 lime, cut into eight thin slices

¼ cup chopped cilantro

Place first eight ingredients in a large soup pot and cook over a low heat for 20 minutes. Squeeze lime juice from each quarter into pot and add two of the rinds to soup (discard other two). Continue cooking for 30 minutes. Remove lime rinds. Portion tortilla strips among bowls and fill with soup. Top each bowl of soup with a lime slice and some cilantro.

Yield: 8 servings

Salads

Inca Grain Salad

▼ ▼ ▼

Quinoa was a staple food of the ancient Incas; its nutlike taste and light consistency has been recently rediscovered by health-food fans. Packed with essential amino acids, quinoa is also a complete protein that both vegans and nonvegetarians can appreciate. It is as easy to cook as rice and can be utilized in as many different ways; I have used it in burrito stuffing, "rice" pudding, and soup, and to thicken fruit pies with equal success.

▲ ▲ ▲

2 cups cooked quinoa	¼ cup olive oil
½ cup chopped cilantro	½ tsp. garlic powder
½ cup chopped watercress	½ tsp. black pepper
½ cup diced green onions	2 tomatoes, quartered
¼ cup sliced black olives	1 lemon, cut into eight slices
½ cup fresh lemon juice	

Mix all ingredients except tomatoes and lemon until well blended, then refrigerate for 3 hours in a glass bowl. Remove from fridge, garnish with tomato wedges and lemon slices and serve.

Yield: Serves 6

Gazpacho Greens

▼ ▼ ▼

This chilled salad is an excellent counterpoint to many of the burritos in this book, especially if the salad is topped with any of the commercially prepared zesty vinaigrette dressings on the market. My own simple dressing has been included below.

▲ ▲ ▲

1 cucumber, peeled, split lengthwise, and chopped

1 bell pepper, seeded and thinly sliced

4 medium tomatoes, diced

1 small purple onion, chopped

1 cup chopped watercress

Lightly toss ingredients in salad bowl and top with as much dressing as desired.

Yield: Serves 4–6

Lemon Vinaigrette

▼ ▼ ▼

½ cup olive oil

Juice from 1 fresh lemon

Salt and pepper to taste

¼ cup red wine vinegar

½ tsp. garlic powder

Combine ingredients in small bowl and mix thoroughly. Pour over salad.

Yield: 1 cup

NOTE: Feel free to experiment with the quantities listed above; some may prefer more garlic, less lemon, or more vinegar and less olive oil. Herbed oil can also be used.

Carrot Bulgur Salad

▼ ▼ ▼

The robust, nutty taste of wheat berries is tempered in its steamed, dried, and cracked form—bulgur. The milder, less chewy texture is a nice contrast to the grated vegetable. This unusual salad was inspired by Middle Eastern tabbouleh and is best served with rather simple lamb or chicken burritos.

▲ ▲ ▲

½ **cup dried bulgur**	6 **carrots, grated**
1 **small red onion, shredded**	1 **cup chopped fresh parsley**
1 **Tb. peanut oil**	1 **tsp. cumin**
½ **tsp. garlic salt**	

Bring 1 cup water to boil in small pot. Add bulgur, stir once; cover, lower heat, and simmer for 35–40 minutes, or until all water has been absorbed. In large bowl combine remaining ingredients. Add bulgur, mix well, cover in plastic wrap, and refrigerate for at least 1 hour before serving.

Yield: 3 cups, 4–6 servings

VARIATION: Add ¼ cup raisins and ¼ cup pineapple chunks packed in juice.

BURRITOS

▼ ▼ ▼

Now, this is the main event: burritos of every flavor and stripe, with recipes that not only celebrate all things Mexican, but wander around the world and back again. Here you'll find recipes that feature fowl, fish, beef, pork, and all manner of vegetables. There are burritos for breakfast, lunch, dinner, and dessert, and there must be at least one burrito here that even your most finicky eater will love.

Try, experiment, and, above all, enjoy!

Basic Traditional Burrito

▼ ▼ ▼

This is as simple as it gets, folks. In the cholesterol-conscious nineties, we shudder at the thought of using lard; however, it is still the favorite choice in eateries north and south of the border. Not only is lard inexpensive and plentiful, but it adds more taste to the beans than does vegetable shortening. For a more healthful alternative, substitute canned black beans for refried in the recipe. Frijoles Negros, as they're commonly called, simply need heating (no lard or refrying in sight!).

On the West Coast, the basic burrito gets dressed up with the addition of cheddar cheese, diced tomatoes, and/or shredded lettuce prior to folding. However, in the Mexican heartland, salad is strictly an on-the-side affair.

▲ ▲ ▲

3 cups refried beans (canned or see recipe page 14)

12 large flour tortillas, warmed

1½ cups Ground Beef Filling (recipe below)

Place 2 Tb. refried beans in the middle of each tortilla. Spread beans—using the back of a spoon so as not to tear the fragile tortilla—from center out, leaving approximately 1 inch uncovered around outer edge of tortilla. Next, spoon 1 heaping Tb. ground beef filling over one-half of beans, making sure to leave exposed edges of each tortilla bare. Fold each burrito in the classic style and serve immediately.

Yield: 12 burritos

Ground Beef Filling

3 Tb. lard or vegetable oil

1 cup finely chopped onion

1 clove garlic, minced

1 lb. ground beef

1 tsp. salt

2 tsp. chili powder

½ tsp. cumin

½ cup tomato paste

Heat lard in large skillet; add onion and garlic and cook until onion is soft and almost transparent. Add beef and seasonings; mix well. Cook until meat is lightly browned, then add tomato paste and cook for 5 minutes, stirring occasionally.

Yield: 2 cups

This is only the beginning, though. From here you can go anywhere, and your imagination is your only limitation.

POULTRY

▼▼▼

Squab Mole Burritos

▼▼▼

Derived from bitter chocolate, classic South American mole (pro-
nounced mole-lay) sauce is most commonly paired with poultry—
chicken, squab, partridge, or duck. The variety is endless. When traveling through the Southwest and Mexico, I learned dozens of recipes
for the rich, dark sauce alone! Every family prides itself on its secret
sauce and few would part with complete instructions. But the Guate-
malan wife of a former employer of mine did not shoo me out of her
Glendale, California, kitchen, and I managed to sneak more than a good
peak at the surprisingly simple squab dish she was preparing for dinner.
In this burrito recipe, grilled boneless chicken breasts can easily be
substituted for the more difficult to find squab (young pigeon). As I'm
not fond of boning poultry (to say the least), I virtually always make
the substitution.

▲▲▲

6 squab, cleaned and patted dry

¼ cup butter

1 Tb. lemon juice

1 tsp. salt

1 tsp. black pepper

12 blue corn tortillas

2 cups cooked brown and wild rice

1 cup grated sharp cheddar cheese

6 green onions, chopped

2 cups Updated Mole Sauce (see recipe page 130), hot

1 cup grated jack cheese

1 cup sliced black olives

Preheat broiler.

Remove the squabs' backbones with knife after bending ribs backward until breastbone cracks. Lay squab flat on broiler rack, skin side down. Melt butter, lemon juice, salt, and pepper in small pan; remove from heat. Using basting brush, spread melted butter over squab. Broil birds for 5 minutes; baste again. Broil birds for another 5 minutes. Turn birds skin side up; baste with melted butter and broil for 5 minutes. Baste birds with remaining melted butter and continue broiling 5–8 minutes, or until birds are thoroughly cooked. Remove from broiler and place on cutting board. Bone squab (flesh will be shredded and crispy skin pieces should be cut into little strips). Discard bones.

Preheat oven to 350 degrees. Portion squab on tortillas; top with rice, cheddar cheese, and onions. Drizzle some mole sauce on mixture and fold classic style. Place seam side down in buttered baking dish; pour over remaining mole sauce. Top with jack cheese and olives and bake for 10 minutes, or until cheese is bubbly. Serve immediately.

Yield: 12 burritos

Thai Chicken
Breakfast Burrito

▼ ▼ ▼

This experiment with refrigerator leftovers turned out to be a Thai-inspired success story.

▲ ▲ ▲

2	Tb. peanut oil	½	cup peanut halves
8	green onions, chopped	¼	cup sunflower seeds
4	green Serrano chilies, diced (include seeds for extra heat)	1	cup creamy peanut butter
		12	eggs, scrambled and broken into bits
2	cups bean sprouts		Cayenne pepper to taste
4	chicken breast halves, cooked and shredded	12	whole wheat tortillas, warmed

Heat oil in large frying pan over medium-high heat; add onions and chilies and cook until onions are translucent. Add bean sprouts and begin stirring; cook for 2 minutes. Add shredded chicken, peanut halves, and sunflower seeds; continue cooking and stirring until chicken is heated thoroughly. Lower heat and mix peanut butter in medium bowl with enough water to make a thick paste. Add peanut butter sauce to pan, stirring to make sure all ingredients are covered. Add egg pieces, season with pepper to taste, turn up heat to medium-high, and continue cooking until peanut sauce begins to bubble, stirring constantly. Spoon mixture onto tortillas, fold pocket-square style, and serve immediately.

Yield: 12 burritos

Tequila Sunrise
Chicken Fajita Burrito

▼ ▼ ▼

This recipe, contributed by Barbara Klein (co-owner and executive chef for Serrano's restaurant in Sedona, Arizona), is an unusually tasty alternative to the usual sautéed chicken burrito. Making use of ingredients such as black beans, grenadine, and orange juice, she's created unforgettable flavor!

▲ ▲ ▲

1 Tb. vegetable oil

1 crookneck squash, sliced

10 mushrooms, sliced

2 whole, skinless, boneless chicken breasts, cut into ½-in. strips

1 cup cooked black beans

1 Tb. grenadine

¼ cup orange juice

⅛ tsp. chili powder

3 Tb. Gold-quality tequila

¼ tsp. garlic powder

1 cup chicken stock

2 Tb. cornstarch

½ cup cold water

1 tomato, diced

6 flour tortillas, warmed

Heat oil in nonstick skillet on medium-high heat. Add squash and mushrooms, cooking until slightly soft; remove from skillet. Add chicken to skillet and cook 6–8 minutes. Return squash and mushrooms to pan; add black beans, grenadine, orange juice, chili powder, tequila, garlic powder, and chicken stock. Lower heat to medium and cook for 5 minutes. In separate bowl, combine cornstarch and water until smooth; add to skillet mixture and stir until thickened. Add tomato and heat through. Portion mixture evenly among tortillas and fold classic style. Serve immediately.

Yield: 6 burritos

Pollo Espinaca
Con Queso Burrito

This recipe makes use of Quick Con Queso (with cheese, in Spanish) Sauce (see page 126). While fresh spinach is much preferred, frozen may be utilized if it is defrosted, well drained, then patted dry.

12 chicken breast halves, skinned and boned

2 Tb. black pepper

1 tsp. chili powder

1 tsp. salt

6 cups cooked fresh spinach (boiled or steamed, then drained)

1½ cups Quick Con Queso Sauce (page 126)

12 corn tortillas, warmed

1 large purple onion, finely chopped

GARNISH

½ cup Quick Con Queso Sauce (page 126)

1 cup sour cream

12 pitted black olives

Preheat broiler.

Sprinkle chicken breasts with pepper, chili powder, and salt; place on broiler rack, broil in oven or grill over charcoal until done, yet still moist and tender.

While chicken is cooking, warm up spinach in one pot and sauce in another. Remove chicken from broiler and slice into thin strips; portion among tortillas. Top chicken with well-drained spinach, some sauce, and chopped onion. Roll classic style and place seam side down on serving plate. Garnish each burrito with cheese sauce, dollop of sour cream, and 1 black olive. Serve immediately.

Yield: 12 burritos

Spicy Yogurt Chicken Burrito

A blend of Indian and Mexican cuisines, this recipe makes use of items commonly found in the refrigerator. It can be served as is for a delicious and simple meal, or additional ingredients and spices can be added for more variety.

1 cup chicken broth	½ cup plain yogurt
1 lemon, quartered	⅓ cup mayonnaise
⅛ tsp. black pepper	6 green onions, chopped
⅛ tsp. paprika	¼ cup chopped fresh parsley
3 whole chicken breasts, skinned, boned, and cut into 1-in. cubes	1 tsp. turmeric
	1 tsp. cumin
1 carrot, diced	1 tsp. cornstarch
1 cup fresh peas (or frozen defrosted)	12 corn tortillas, warmed

Combine broth, lemon, pepper, and paprika in large frying pan and bring to boil over medium-high heat. Add chicken, carrot, and peas; lower heat and simmer for 15 minutes, or until chicken is thoroughly done.

While chicken mixture is simmering, combine the yogurt, mayonnaise, onions, parsley, turmeric, cumin, and cornstarch in saucepan. Remove 4 Tb. of chicken broth from frying pan and add to contents of saucepan. Cover remaining chicken and broth mixture to keep hot (heat should be on lowest setting). Stirring constantly, heat yogurt mixture in saucepan over medium heat until it thickens and starts to boil; cover and remove from heat. Using a slotted spoon, ladle the chicken and vegetables onto the tortillas. Spoon heated yogurt mixture on top of chicken and vegetables; fold filled tortillas pocket-square style and serve seam side down.

Yield: 12 burritos

VARIATION: Use one-half of yogurt mixture inside of burritos; when folded, place in baking dish. Pour remaining sauce on top and sprinkle with grated Parmesan cheese and more green onions. Broil for 3 minutes, or until cheese is golden brown.

Chilled Smoked Turkey Burrito

An elegant appetizer or popular party item, this burrito looks like a colorful pinwheel when cut on the bias and fanned out around a small bowl of red salsa. Simple to make, it can be whipped together in minutes for unexpected company.

2 jalapeños, seeded and minced

8 oz. firm cream cheese

¼ cup sour cream

4 oz. green or red chili salsa

3 ripe avocados, peeled

2 Tb. lemon juice

½ tsp. onion powder

¼ tsp. pepper

1 lb. smoked turkey, cut paper thin

6 flour tortillas, warmed

Salsa or corn relish

In small bowl, mix together jalapeños, cream cheese, sour cream, and salsa until well blended; reserve. In another small bowl, mash avocado with lemon juice until fairly smooth; add onion powder and pepper and continue mashing until smooth. Thickly slather tortillas with jalapeño-cheese mixture out to edge. Top mixture with turkey slices, then slather avocado mash on top of turkey. Roll up tortillas like jelly rolls; slice burritos on bias (space cuts about ¾ inch apart) to make pinwheel shapes. Serve with salsa or corn relish.

Yield: 6 burritos, approximately 36 pinwheels

Amaranth-Chicken Burrito

▼ ▼ ▼

The ancient Aztecs used amaranth grain as a dietary staple since it is naturally high in protein as well as other nutrients. Ground into flour, it was baked into flat loaves and offered in religious ceremonies as well as consumed by the Indians themselves on a daily basis. Currently available in health-food stores, amaranth is used in place of rice as a pilaf or soup ingredient. The Anasazi bean spread recipe was created and provided by Arrowhead Mills.

▲ ▲ ▲

3 boneless, skinless chicken breasts

1 crookneck squash, cut into ¼-in.-thick slices

1 medium zucchini, cut into ¼-in.-thick slices

1 carrot, cut into ¼-in.-thick slices

1 cup cooked Anasazi beans

½ medium onion, diced

1 stalk celery, chopped

¼ cup tofu, drained

1 Tb. olive oil

1½ tsp. tamari

1 tsp. chili powder

½ tsp. oregano

½ tsp. basil

¼ tsp. garlic powder

12 blue corn tortillas, warmed

1 cup amaranth, cooked and drained

½ cup grated soy cheese

Salsa, at room temperature

Broil chicken breasts, both sides, until cooked; remove from broiler and shred meat. Set aside. Steam squash, zucchini, and carrot. Using a food processor, blend Anasazi beans, onion, celery, tofu, oil, tamari, chili powder, oregano, basil, and garlic powder until smooth and creamy. Portion bean spread evenly among tortillas; top with shredded chicken, steamed vegetables, amaranth, and grated soy cheese. Fold filled tortillas pocket-square style and place on microwavable plates, seam side down. Put in microwave and heat for 2 minutes. Garnish with salsa and serve immediately.

Yield: 12 burritos

NOTE: For those of you who have not succumbed to the lure of the microwave oven, simply wrap the burritos in aluminum foil and place in a preheated 350-degree oven 20–25 minutes to ensure that all ingredients are heated equally prior to serving.

Sautéed Chicken-Guacamole Burritos

▼ ▼ ▼

This simple yet savory burrito takes only 30 minutes to make and can easily be expanded to accommodate unexpected dinner guests with the addition of a portion of cooked rice to each burrito.

▲ ▲ ▲

- 1 tsp. salt
- 1 tsp. black pepper
- 1 tsp. paprika
- 6 chicken breast halves, boned, skinned, and cut into 1-in. cubes
- ¼ cup butter
- 2 medium onions, sliced and pushed into rings

- 1 cup sliced mushrooms
- 1 cup canned corn, rinsed and drained
- 2 tsp. fresh lime juice
- 1½ cups Uncle Fred's Guacamole (see page 121)
- 12 corn tortillas, warmed

Sprinkle salt, pepper, and paprika on chicken cubes. Melt butter in large frying pan on medium-high heat; add onions and mushrooms, and cook until onions are lightly golden. Add corn, chicken cubes, and lime juice. Lower heat to medium and sauté mixture until chicken is thoroughly done and onions are golden brown. Remove from heat, cover to keep warm. Thickly spread guacamole onto tortillas; using a slotted spoon, portion chicken-vegetable mixture on each tortilla. Fold classic style and serve immediately.

Yield: 12 burritos

Post-Christmas Burrito

▼ ▼ ▼

There are many possible variations on this basic recipe. Most Southwestern American and Mexican cooks prepare some form of candied carrots (or sweet potatoes or yams) and turkey (or chicken or duck or goose) for the holiday meal. Often pearl onions are baked along with the fowl, and raisins can be found in either the carrot dish or in the stuffing itself. But what to do with excess ingredients and/or leftovers? By reading this recipe the inspired home chef can learn how to incorporate his or her own holiday remains into a refreshing meal.

▲ ▲ ▲

¼ **cup butter**

2 **lb. cooked chicken breast, duck, goose, or turkey, cut into bite-size pieces**

2 **carrots, yams, or sweet potatoes, cut into ¼-in.-thick slices**

1 **cup (8 oz.) fresh or canned pearl onions**

¾ **cup seedless golden or brown raisins**

1 **tsp. salt**

1 **tsp. black pepper**

½ **tsp. cayenne pepper**

1 **tsp. thyme**

½ **tsp. rosemary**

½ **cup white wine (Chardonnay is good)**

¼ **cup heavy cream**

12 **flour tortillas, warmed**

Melt the butter in large pan over medium-high heat. Add the cooked poultry, carrots, yams, or sweet potatoes, onions, and raisins. Stirring constantly, let brown for 3 minutes; add salt, pepper, cayenne, thyme, and rosemary. Lower heat to medium and slowly pour in wine, stirring to blend well. Turn heat to low, cover, and simmer for 45 minutes. (Carrots should be done al dente—firm but tender). Remove pan from heat and stir in cream; return pan to heat, stirring constantly, for 1 minute (sauce should be warm, not bubbling). Using a large spoon, portion solid ingredients among tortillas; fold pocket-square style, drizzle with remaining sauce, and serve seam side down.

Yield: 12 burritos

Chicken-Eggplant
Goulash Burrito

▼ ▼ ▼

To an American of Middle European descent, goulash is a nice way of saying "leftovers." Like burritos, a good goulash is often created from the hodgepodge remnants of the week's previous meals: a piece of pork shoulder, a few carrots, some parsley potatoes, a handful of peas, etc. The secret to good goulash, and beautiful burritos, is in the way the disparate ingredients are bound together and seasoned. This recipe was inspired equally by peering into my pathetically stocked fridge on a very gray, blustery Saturday morning in 1982, and fond memories of the major miracles my "Nana" (paternal grandmother) performed in her walk-up New York City apartment kitchen. She was a simple woman who could create culinary magic on a moment's notice with the most unlikely of leftovers and a smidgen of sour cream. She inspires me still.

▲ ▲ ▲

1 small eggplant, cut into bite-size cubes

1½ tsp. salt

¼ cup butter

1 clove garlic, crushed

1 small white onion, sliced into rings

6 oz. boned and skinned duck breast, or 4 boned and skinned chicken breast halves, cut into bite-size cubes

10 medium mushrooms, sliced

1 tsp. black pepper

⅛ tsp. cayenne pepper

1 tsp. paprika

2 tsp. lemon juice

½ cup sour cream

½ tsp. Dijon mustard

12 tortillas, warmed

Sprinkle eggplant with 1 tsp. salt, place in colander, and let drain for 30 minutes; pat dry with paper towels. In large frying pan, melt butter over medium heat; add eggplant, garlic, onion, and poultry. Cook 10–12 minutes, stirring occasionally, until eggplant is light brown and poultry is almost done. Add mushrooms and continue cooking 3–4 minutes, by which time poultry should be done. Lower heat, add seasonings and lemon juice, stirring to make sure eggplant and poultry cubes are coated. In small bowl, mix sour cream and mustard thoroughly; add this mixture to contents of pan, stirring constantly until all ingredients are well blended. Simmer 5–8 minutes, stirring constantly so mixture will not stick or boil. Using slotted spoon, portion mixture among tortillas and fold in classic style. Serve seam side down and garnish with dollop of sour cream-mustard sauce.

Yield: 12 burritos

Dixie Chicken Burrito

▼　▼　▼

Two staples of the Deep South—okra and fried chicken—are the inspiration for this simple recipe. Diced skinned and boned chicken breast and defrosted okra are time-saving ingredients for those in a hurry. The groats can be made the night before and refrigerated.

▲　▲　▲

½ **cup barley groats**	1 **tsp. salt**
4 **chicken breasts, boned and skinned**	1 **medium yellow onion, chopped**
3 **Tb. butter**	Two **10-oz. packages frozen okra, thawed and drained**
1 **tsp. cumin**	
1 **tsp. cayenne pepper**	12 **corn tortillas, warmed**

Boil 1 cup water in a small pot; add groats, cover, lower heat, and simmer for 1 hour (grains should be whole with a chewy texture, not mushy). Cut chicken into bite-size pieces; sauté in melted butter using large, deep skillet. When chicken is almost done, add remaining ingredients and cook for 10 minutes, stirring well. Chicken should be cooked through (test sample pieces during cooking process). Place tortillas flat on board; spoon out groats (2–3 Tb. per tortilla, depending upon size). Portion chicken-okra mixture evenly among tortillas; roll up jelly-roll style and serve seam side down.

Yield: 12 burritos

Chicken Parmigiana Burrito

▼ ▼ ▼

Chicken parmigiana was one of my most favorite childhood dishes; I could be persuaded into any chore if this was the reward (hey, some kids love ice cream . . . I was different, okay?). It's still a reward for me, and I have enjoyed many versions of it. In a pinch, I have been known to purchase frozen breaded chicken breast patties, top with Ragu marinara sauce, lots of mozzarella, and a hint of Parmesan cheese; of course, I wouldn't tell this to any of my chef friends, but we must have *some* secrets, after all, yes?

▲ ▲ ▲

1 tsp. salt	1 large tomato, diced
1 tsp. black pepper	2 cups Homemade Tomato Sauce (see page 128)
2 tsp. Italian seasoning	12 corn tortillas, warmed
12 chicken breast halves, boned and skinned	2 cups grated mozzarella cheese
2 tsp. olive oil	¼ cup grated Parmesan cheese
1 large onion, diced	
1 cup sliced mushrooms	

Preheat broiler.

Sprinkle salt, pepper, and Italian seasoning on both sides of each chicken breast half; place on rack and broil for 10 minutes on each side, or until chicken is moist yet done in the middle.

While chicken is broiling, heat oil over medium-high heat in large frying pan; add onion and mushrooms, and fry until onions are translucent. Add tomato and 1½ cups tomato sauce; let boil, then lower heat. Cut chicken breasts into bite-size pieces, add to tomato sauce mixture, and simmer for 15 minutes, stirring occasionally. Portion mixture among tortillas, fold jelly-roll style, and place seam side down in nonstick casserole dish or buttered baking pan. Cover burritos with remaining tomato sauce, top with mozzarella, and sprinkle with Parmesan. Place in broiler and cook until cheese turns bubbly and begins to brown; serve immediately.

Yield: 12 saucy burritos

South African Burrito

▼ ▼ ▼

Adapted from a recipe in the *African News Cookbook* (Viking, 1985) this coconut chicken entrée is luxuriously spiced and sure to satisfy the most jaded palate.

▲ ▲ ▲

One 3-lb. chicken, cut into pieces

1 cup grated coconut

½ tsp. ground cloves

2 cardamom pods

1 tsp. ground cinnamon

1 tsp. poppy seeds

¼ tsp. cumin

¼ tsp. ground ginger

1½ tsp. cayenne pepper

1 tsp. minced garlic

2 Tb. heavy cream

2 medium onions, diced

¼ cup butter

2 oz. slivered almonds

12 pistachios, shelled

6 oz. can water chestnuts

12 large flour tortillas, warmed

Wash and drain the chicken pieces. Puree coconut, spices, garlic, and cream in blender; reserve. In a large skillet, fry the onions in butter until just golden; remove onions from pan and reserve butter. Brown chicken in same skillet.

Preheat oven to 350 degrees.

In a large baking dish combine everything except tortillas; bake for 45 minutes, or until chicken is done. Place chicken pieces on cutting board and remove and discard all bones. Shred chicken and return to baking pan. Spread tortillas on clean board and portion coconut-chicken mixture evenly among them; use classic fold, and serve immediately.

Yield: 12 burritos

Griddled Ancho
Chicken Burrito

If you do not have a pancake griddle, use a frying pan lightly sprayed with PAM vegetable oil to heat chilies, tomatoes, and tomatillos.

ANCHO SALSA

- 3 **mulato chilies (dried anchos)**
- 4 **sprigs fresh cilantro**
- 2 **medium red tomatoes**
- 3 **tomatillos, husked**
- 2 **Tb. pepitos (toasted pumpkin seeds)**

BURRITOS

- 4 **chicken breasts, boned and skinned**
- 1 **tsp. vegetable oil**
- 1 **medium zucchini, cut in ¼-in. slices**
- 1 **cup diced cauliflower**
- 8 **blue corn tortillas, warmed**
- 8 **oz. feta cheese**
- **Sour cream (optional)**

Set griddle thermostat to high and toast chilies until soft. Remove chilies from griddle; seed and remove membrane from them. Place chilies in blender jar with cilantro; process until pasty (add water, if necessary, in 1 tsp. portions until desired consistency is achieved). Cut tomatoes and tomatillos in half; place skin side down on hot griddle and sear 2—3 minutes. Add tomatoes, tomatillos, and pepitos to chili mixture. Process ingredients until smooth; reserve.

Cut chicken into 1-inch cubes. Pour oil onto hot griddle; add chicken. Add zucchini and cauliflower to chicken on griddle; fry, stirring constantly, until chicken is cooked through. Lay warmed tortillas on board, spread thick layer of ancho salsa on each. Crumble 1 oz. feta cheese on each tortilla, add chicken-vegetable mixture equally. Fold each burrito pocket-square style, garnish with remaining salsa and dollop of sour cream if desired. Serve immediately.

Yield: 8 burritos

Chicken Satay Burrito

▼ ▼ ▼

When it comes to Thai food, I must admit a weakness for satay: those deliciously grilled bits of chicken served with scrumptious peanut sauce! My only gripe is that there's never enough peanut sauce to go around, so I decided to learn how to make it myself and create a burrito that perfectly portions this savory sauce with other typically Thai ingredients. I inquired at several Los Angeles restaurants regarding satay sauce ingredients and received basically the same information. Appreciation is given to Toi, Chan Dara, and Chao Praya restaurants for their help.

▲ ▲ ▲

6 whole chicken breasts, boned and skinned

½ cup soy sauce

Juice of 4 limes

½ cup white wine

2 cloves garlic, crushed

2 bay leaves

2 Tb. peanut oil

4 cups bean sprouts

8 green onions, chopped

SATAY SAUCE

1 lb. fresh raw peanuts, shelled

2 tsp. chili powder

3 cloves garlic

1 tsp. salt

1 onion, chopped

4 Tb. peanut oil

¼ cup water

1 Tb. brown sugar

1 tsp. soy sauce

2 Tb. lemon juice

12 flour tortillas, warmed

Cut chicken breasts into thin strips. Mix soy sauce, lime juice, wine, and crushed garlic in medium bowl; add chicken strips and mix well. Add bay leaves, cover bowl with plastic wrap, place in refrigerator, and marinate overnight.

Place 2 Tb. peanut oil in large wok or frying pan over medium-high heat. Remove bay leaves from chicken mixture, pour out marinade, then place chicken in wok. Stirring constantly, add bean sprouts and green onions. Cook until chicken is lightly browned on edges and sprouts are soft. Turn off heat, cover, and keep warm.

To make satay sauce, put the peanuts in blender jar with chili powder, garlic cloves, salt, onion, and 2 Tb. peanut oil. Blend into a smooth paste, adding enough of the ¼ cup water to keep ingredients from sticking to jar. Heat remaining 2 Tb. peanut oil in medium pan over medium-high heat; pour peanut sauce into pan and stir. Reduce heat to medium-low and cook the paste for 3 minutes, stirring constantly. Stir in the remaining water and continue cooking until sauce is thick and smooth. Add brown sugar, soy sauce, and lemon juice; stir well and remove from heat. Spread sauce onto tortillas; portion stir-fried chicken-vegetable mixture on each tortilla, and top with more sauce. Fold burritos pocket-square style and serve immediately.

Yield: 12 burritos

Pollo Fria Picnic Burrito

▼ ▼ ▼

A delightfully refreshing alternative to sandwiches, this cold chicken burrito by Barbara Klein (co-owner and executive chef of Serrano's restaurant in Sedona, Arizona) is not cooked but simply assembled in minutes—perfect for those quick summer getaways!

▲ ▲ ▲

6 flour tortillas

8 oz. softened cream cheese

7 oz. can diced green chilies, drained

6 green onions, chopped

1 medium tomato, chopped

¼ cup minced cilantro

7 oz. can pitted black olives, sliced

2 cups cooked, shredded chicken

8 romaine lettuce leaves, shredded

1 cup shredded cheddar cheese

¼ cup chopped pecans

Lay out tortillas on board and spread evenly with softened cream cheese (be gentle or tortillas will shred). Portion remaining ingredients over cream cheese and layer in order given above. Fold classic style and press firmly as you roll up each burrito. Wrap tightly in plastic wrap and chill for at least 4 hours.

Yield: 6 burritos

Quick-'N'-Easy
Chicken-Broccoli Burrito

▼ ▼ ▼

Frozen broccoli, canned soup, and leftover chicken help this dish come out perfectly at lightning speed—great when you've come home late from work or your children have brought home unexpected guests. It's not gourmet, but it is hearty and wholesome. Of course, fresh ingredients will make for better burritos.

▲ ▲ ▲

One 10-oz. package frozen broccoli, chopped, or 1 cup freshly steamed

One 10¾-oz. can condensed cream-of-chicken soup

2 cups cubed or thinly sliced cooked chicken

⅓ cup grated Parmesan cheese

One 15-oz. can pitted black Spanish olives, drained and sliced, or 1½ cups pitted and sliced fresh olives

8 flour tortillas

1 cup shredded cheddar cheese

Cook broccoli according to directions; drain, then place in large mixing bowl. Add soup, chicken, Parmesan and one-half of the sliced black olives; mix well.

Preheat oven to 350 degrees.

Place tortillas flat on counter or board, fill with chicken mixture, and roll up, using a pocket-square fold. Place seam side down on greased shallow baking dish; bake for 10 minutes. Remove and sprinkle with shredded cheddar and other half of black olives. Bake for 5 minutes or until cheddar is bubbly. Serve immediately.

Yield: 8 burritos

NOTE: If no cooked chicken leftovers are available, simply bake 4 boned and skinned chicken breasts in a preheated 350-degree oven for 20 minutes, or until chicken is thoroughly cooked.

VARIATION: Soak chicken breasts in lime juice overnight, then grill, making sure chicken is at least 2 in. from flame or heating element.

Chicken-Guacamole Burrito

In less than 15 minutes, these simple yet tasty burritos can be assembled utilizing leftover chicken. For best results, follow directions for marinated chicken breasts (recipe below).

2 cups shredded cooked chicken	1 large tomato, diced
4 large flour tortillas	1 cup Uncle Fred's Guacamole (see page 121)

Spoon ½ cup chicken each tortilla; spread evenly over surface, leaving 1 in. bare around edge. Sprinkle diced tomato in a line down center of each tortilla. Spoon guacamole over tomatoes. Wrap, using the classic fold, and serve.

Yield: 4 large burritos

VARIATION: Sprinkle grated cheddar cheese over each wrapped burrito, pop in microwave for 1 minute, or until cheese melts, and serve.

Marinated Chicken Breasts

4 chicken breast halves, boned and skinned	1 tsp. chili powder
Juice of 6 limes	1 tsp. cayenne pepper

Place breast halves in plastic bag or in small casserole dish with a cover. Pour juice over breasts, sprinkle with chili powder and pepper. Let marinate in refrigerator overnight. Remove breasts from marinade; grill or bake in preheated 350-degree oven 15—20 minutes (or until chicken is thoroughly done). Shred chicken by hand and use in burrito filling mixture.

Yield: 2 cups

SEAFOOD

▼▼▼

While visiting San Francisco during my college years, I inadvertently wandered into an almost mystical alleyway in the Chinatown section. No garish neon signs or flapping paper banners boldly proclaiming the best restaurants here; only the indescribably delicious aroma of dozens of sizzling hot woks, all overflowing with a variety of exotic delights. I boldly peered through the open wooden doors as I walked, savoring the scents and sights of butterfish, tiger prawn, squid, and abalone all being tossed with garden greens into hissing sesame oil. This was no place for tourists, and from the way the ancient men in baggy undershirts were regarding me, I figured it was time to flee. When I remember the city by the bay, I don't think of Ghiaradelli Square or Coit Tower or even the majestic bridge itself . . . I simply close my eyes and let my tastebuds tango to the tantalizing tease of sizzling seafood done Asian style.

Mixed Seafood Burrito

▼ ▼ ▼

2 Tb. sesame oil

6 oz. can diced clams, drained

6 oz. crabmeat (fresh, if possible)

6 oz. cooked and peeled medium-size shrimp

6 oz. squid, diced into 1-in. cubes

¼ cup chopped green onions

½ cup celery, bias cut into bite-size pieces

1 cup bean sprouts

2 Tb. rice wine or white wine

1 tsp. soy sauce

1 tsp. white pepper

12 flour tortillas, warmed

Lemon wedges

Heat wok or large deep-frying pan; add sesame oil. When oil sputters, add seafood and begin stir-frying. After squid has turned a light golden brown, add onions and celery; continue stir-frying until celery is barely crisp (al dente), then add bean sprouts, rice or white wine, soy sauce, and pepper, stirring vigorously to make sure all ingredients are coated. Turn off heat and portion onto tortillas using a slotted spoon. Fold in classic style and serve seam side down. Garnish with lemon wedges.

Yield: 12 burritos

VARIATION: Thicken the wine-soy sauce mixture with a little cornstarch (approximately ½ teaspoon) and add a pinch of freshly grated ginger; serve burritos with side of plain brown rice drizzled with hoisin sauce.

The Nutty Cabo San Lucas Swordfish Burrito

▼ ▼ ▼

Okay, so everybody goes a little nutty their first time down at the point. The two Cabos are filled with temptation—the finest tequila, the sweetest fruit, the bluest water, the whitest sand . . . and yes, some of the best deep-sea fishing known on the North American continent. You can't walk into a cantina without being regaled with fish stories; marlin the size of a "Cad-dilly-ac" are common. It seems like everyone has lost one at least once in Cabo. The recipe below is dedicated to all those Hemingway-esque adventurers who have sought the great fish south of the border.

▲ ▲ ▲

Four 1-in.-thick swordfish steaks (1½–2 lb.)
Juice of 4 limes
 1 tsp. cayenne pepper
½ tsp. black pepper
½ tsp. salt
¼ cup butter
 1 cup fresh corn kernels
 1 Serrano chili pepper, seeded and finely diced

¼ cup slivered almonds
¼ cup roughly crushed hazelnuts
¼ cup roughly crushed Brazil nuts
12 corn tortillas, warm
Sour cream
12 walnut halves

Marinate swordfish steaks in plastic bag overnight in lime juice, cayenne pepper, black pepper, and salt. Preheat broiler or prepare outdoor grill, remove fish from bag, and broil until firm; it should be white with dark brown scoremarks. Reserve, and keep warm. Melt butter in small pot over medium heat; add corn, chili pepper, and all nuts except walnut halves. Stir until all ingredients are covered with butter and hot; cover and remove from heat. Dice swordfish into 1-inch cubes and portion equally among tortillas; add corn-nut mixture. Fold jelly-roll style, garnish with a dollop of sour cream topped with a walnut half.

Yield: 12 burritos

Nigerian Shrimp Burrito

While writing my Master's thesis, I struck up the acquaintanceship of several exchange students from this African nation. Their strict adherence to traditional dress impressed me, as most other foreign students had readily adopted the torn jeans and T-shirt look of Hollywood. I loved the bright colors and graceful stylings of their voluminous robes as much as their easy laughter and natural good humor. I also came to love their food. One of the students, who claimed to be some kind of prince, would receive shipments of culinary "necessities" from home once a week. He would then prepare a feast for a select few of us that was not easily forgotten. This dish is adapted from one of those inspired recipes. I've forgotten this generous man's name, but my tastebuds will always be grateful to him and his family.

1 **eggplant, peeled and cubed**
Salt
6 **Tb. peanut oil**
2 **large onions, sliced and pushed into rings**
4 **tomatoes, seeded and diced**
3 **Tb. tomato puree**
3 **Tb. black pepper**
1¼ **cups chicken stock**
36 **large shrimp, shelled and cut into 1-in. pieces**
8 **oz. can corn, rinsed and drained**
12 **corn tortillas, warmed**
1 **cup chopped cilantro**

Sprinkle eggplant with salt; let drain, then pat dry with a paper towel. Place eggplant in a large frying pan; cover with water and boil for 3 minutes. Lower heat and continue cooking for 15 minutes, or until eggplant is very soft. Drain eggplant in collander, then place in large mixing bowl. Mash eggplant until smooth and pulpy; set aside. Heat oil in large frying pan over medium-high heat; add onions and fry until golden. Lower heat slightly and add tomatoes, tomato puree, eggplant mash, and chicken stock, stirring well. Cook 15 minutes, or until mixture has thickened, stirring occasionally. Add shrimp and corn; continue cooking until shrimp are pink and thoroughly done, about 5 minutes, stirring occasionally. Spoon mixture onto tortillas, sprinkle with cilantro, fold classic style, and serve immediately.

Yield: 12 burritos

Spicy Prawn and Squash Burrito

▼ ▼ ▼

Jumbo tiger prawns are among my favorite feasts; I have enjoyed them stir-fried, baked, broiled, grilled, boiled, and steamed. What I like about them besides their meaty consistency is their ability to soak up whatever seasonings come their way, allowing for an unlimited number of culinary creations. This dish is essentially simple; the kicker is in the number and type of chili peppers used. While not hot enough to blow out one's tastebuds, it will definitely warm the cockles of one's heart.

▲ ▲ ▲

3 Tb. vegetable oil

1 medium onion, diced

1 clove garlic, crushed

3 green Serrano chilies, seeded and finely diced

2 Tb. soy sauce

¼ tsp. chili powder

¼ tsp. black pepper

24 fresh prawns, shelled and cut into 1-in. pieces

2 crookneck squash, cut into ¼-in.-thick slices

1 large zucchini, cut into ¼-in.-thick slices

12 blue corn tortillas, warmed

Heat oil in a large frying pan over medium-high heat; add onion, garlic, and chilies. Stir occasionally and cook until onion begins to turn golden. Add soy sauce, chili powder, and black pepper; stir well. Add remaining ingredients and continue cooking, stirring frequently until squash is tender, about 8 minutes. Divide mixture evenly among tortillas; figure 2 prawns per portion. Fold classic style and serve immediately.

Yield: 12 burritos

Broiled Oyster Burrito

Seemingly one of my more wacky creations, it actually begins with a classic French recipe called Huitres Gratinées à la Crème, which I helped a Parisian disk jockey prepare for a dinner party in 1974 in Redlands, California. Joel was a wonderful chef, an inspired teacher, and an even better host; he also forgave my pitiful attempts to speak with his Canadian guests utilizing my pidgin French, for which I am entirely grateful. They found me amusing and charming; I found the evening inspiration for this delicious dish!

1 Tb. vegetable oil
1 tsp. white wine
1 medium onion, diced
2 celery stalks, finely diced
¼ cup chopped fresh parsley
1 tsp. white pepper

48 oysters
(if canned, rinse well and drain)
1 cup heavy cream
⅓ cup butter, melted
¾ cup grated Parmesan cheese
12 flour tortillas, warmed

Heat vegetable oil over medium-high heat in medium frying pan; when sizzling, add wine, onion, celery, parsley, and pepper. Sauté, stirring frequently, until celery and onion are both soft but not mushy. Remove onion and celery using slotted spoon and keep warm.

Preheat broiler; lightly grease a shallow baking dish (using butter or spray-on PAM) and arrange oysters in one layer in dish. Drizzle a little cream over each one, making sure all cream is used and each oyster is evenly covered. Now drizzle melted butter over oysters in same way. Sprinkle oysters evenly with Parmesan and place baking dish on broiler rack. Broil oysters 4–5 minutes, or until the mixture is bubbling and starting to turn brown. Quickly remove from broiler and place four oysters plus sauce on each tortilla; divide celery-onion-parsley mixture among them evenly. Fold classic style and serve immediately seam side down.

Yield: 12 burritos

Broiled Halibut with
Lemon Sauce Burrito

A simple, elegant supper, these burritos have a delicate flavor and delightful texture.

6 **halibut steaks (about 2½ lbs.)**

¼ **cup butter, melted**

2 **Tb. minced chives**

1 **medium turnip, cut into ½-in. cubes**

1 **carrot, cut into ¼-in. slices**

1 **small jicama, cut into ½-in. cubes**

1 **Tb. butter**

1 **clove garlic, crushed**

1 **Tb. flour**

1¼ **cups milk**

1 **Tb. minced chervil**

½ **tsp. thyme**

¼ **tsp. black pepper**

¼ **tsp. salt**

1 **tsp. grated lemon rind**

1 **Tb. light cream**

1 **tsp. lemon juice**

12 **whole wheat tortillas, warmed**

Sprigs of parsley (optional)

Place broiler rack approximately 4 inches from heating element; preheat broiler. Place halibut on rack; brush with melted butter and sprinkle on half of the chives. Broil for 5 minutes, then turn; brush with more melted butter and sprinkle on remaining chives. Continue broiling until fish is firm, yet lightly flaky when tested with fork.

While fish is broiling, steam turnip, carrot, and jicama; keep warm in steamer until ready to assemble burritos. To make sauce, melt 1 Tb. butter over medium heat in medium saucepan; add garlic and continue cooking for 3 minutes. Remove pan from heat, stir in flour gradually until a smooth paste has formed. Add milk, stirring constantly; mix in chervil, thyme, pepper, salt, and lemon rind. Return saucepan to heat and bring sauce to a boil, stirring constantly so it doesn't stick. Reduce heat to low, cover pan, and simmer 12 minutes, stirring occasionally. Stir in cream and lemon juice and continue cooking, stirring constantly, for 3 more minutes. Turn off heat and keep warm while assembling burritos.

Remove fish from broiler and cut into bite-size cubes. Portion fish equally among tortillas, add vegetables, and pour on enough sauce to just cover burrito ingredients (do not smother). Fold filled tortillas classic style and place seam side down on plates. Drizzle with remaining sauce and serve immediately. Garnish with sprig of fresh parsley, if desired.

Yield: 12 burritos

Mussels–Lemon Rice Burrito

Let's face it, steamed mussels are a bore; rarely above the Rio Grande do you find a truly exciting recipe for these tempting morsels. When I was rafting the Brown's Canyon section of the Arkansas River (and admiring three 14,000+-foot peaks in the distance), a companion adventurer told me of a white-water river in Mexico and the delicious lemon mussel dish he enjoyed at the end of his excursion down the rapids. From the details he parted with, and more than a little creative license on my part, I was able to replicate the dish and have included it below. When purchasing mussels, make sure that the shells are closed and not broken. Prepare mussels for cooking by scraping off any mud or debris with a butter knife, then scrubbing the shells with a stiff bristle brush. If the mussels have little beards protruding from one end, remove these carefully with the tip of a sharp knife. Mussels should be soaked in cold water for at least 1 hour prior to cooking, then drained.

½ cup butter

1 tsp. thyme

1 tsp. rosemary

½ tsp. salt

½ tsp. white pepper

1 bay leaf

½ cup finely chopped fresh parsley

2 medium onions, diced

1 cup freshly squeezed lemon juice

5 qt. mussels, cleaned

2 Tb. flour

1 cup long-grain rice, cooked

24 asparagus spears, steamed and kept warm

12 flour tortillas, warmed

Melt ¼ cup butter in a large frying pan over medium heat; add thyme, rosemary, salt, pepper, bay leaf, parsley, and onions. Cook, stirring occasionally, until onions are soft and almost translucent. Add lemon juice, stir; increase heat and add mussels. Cook for 3 minutes or until the shells open, making sure to shake and stir the pan constantly (beware of shaking too hard and splattering liquid on hands!). Remove pan from heat; find and discard bay leaf. Using tongs, remove mussels and let cool sufficiently so that meat can be removed from shells; discard shells. (Be sure to strain the liquid in the pan before using it for your sauce; the mussels may cough up a little sand when they open.)

Melt remaining butter in small pan over medium heat. Remove pan from heat and gradually add flour, stirring until a paste has formed. Replace big frying pan with mussel liquid on stove over medium heat; gradually add paste, stirring constantly until sauce has thickened, 3–5 minutes. Add mussels and cooked rice to frying pan; lower heat and simmer for 3 minutes, stirring frequently. Remove pan from heat. Place two warm asparagus spears next to each other in middle of each tortilla; top with mussel—lemon rice mixture. Fold burritos classic style and serve immediately.

Yield:12 burritos

Santa Fe Salmon Burrito
with Shrimp Spread

Exploring the Four Corners area of the southwestern United States has always been a pleasure for me; there is so much to see and do! Monument Valley Navajo Tribal Park, with its several thousand square miles of isolated sandstone monoliths; Canyon de Chelly National Monument, with its Pueblo-built apartment-style rock homes built into the sides of mountains over one thousand years ago; and the geological formation known as Shiprock in New Mexico, which is the basalt core of an old volcano, and seems to float majestically over 1700 feet above the valley floor. One of the finest salmon steaks I've ever enjoyed was at the La Fonda Hotel in the early eighties; mesquite grilled, it was topped with a jalapeño sauce that was incomparable. While real mesquite grilling is out of reach for most cooks, we can duplicate the taste with a little inventiveness in the kitchen. How's your BBQ IQ?

▲ ▲ ▲

SHRIMP SPREAD

8 oz. firm cream cheese	1 Tb. Worcestershire sauce, or A–1 for poultry
2 Tb. ranch dressing	
1 Tb. minced onion	2 Tb. butter, melted
1 Tb. minced garlic	12 oz. precooked popcorn shrimp

BURRITOS

¼ cup butter	¼ tsp. garlic powder
2 Tb. lemon juice	2 lb. salmon steaks
2 Tb. chopped cilantro	12 flour tortillas, warmed
½ tsp. tarragon	Lime wedges
½ tsp. whole sea salt	Pitted black olives, sliced

Thoroughly mix together all ingredients except shrimp. Lightly fold in shrimp, cover bowl with plastic wrap, and set aside. Do not refrigerate unless you're not using immediately.

Get coals of barbecue ready. Melt butter in small saucepan with lemon juice, cilantro, and seasonings. Place salmon steaks on grill and brush seasoned butter on top side. Cook for 6 minutes, flip fish over, baste with seasoned butter and cook for 5 more minutes. Baste fish again and continue cooking until fish flakes easily when tested with fork.

Cover tortillas with chunky shrimp spread leaving 1-in. border around edges. Remove salmon from grill and cut into 1-in. cubes; place cubes on tortillas, roll classic style, and serve immediately. Garnish with lime wedges and sliced black olives.

Yield: 12 burritos

Shark Burrito

▼ ▼ ▼

Reading about the Bahamas inspired this recipe. By integrating local fish with West African cuisine, a new taste sensation was born. These very simple and relatively inexpensive components yield a delightful change of pace for the average Norte Americano diner. Any shark fillet can be used, but I prefer thresher shark for its firm but flaky texture and ''meaty'' taste. I've avoided adding lemon to this recipe because it would tamper with the natural sweetness of the sweet potatos and onion. Feel free to substitute peeled, boiled, and mashed yams if you can get any fresh from the grocery store; this is what the islanders use.

▲ ▲ ▲

12 oz. can sweet potatos, drained and mashed	1 large red onion, sliced and pushed into rings
2 Tb. butter	2 lb. shark steaks
1 tsp. salt	12 corn tortillas, warmed
1 tsp. cayenne pepper	

Warm the sweet potato pulp in a small saucepan over low heat, stirring occasionally. Melt the butter in a medium frying pan; when frothy add the salt, pepper, and onion rings, sautéing until rings are soft but not translucent. Keep butter and onions warm.

Preheat broiler, place shark on broiler rack. With a brush, baste top sides of steaks with seasoned butter. Place no more than 4 in. under broiler element and cook 6–7 minutes, or until lightly browned. Turn over and baste with more seasoned butter; continue cooking until fish flakes when tested with fork. Remove fish and cut into 1-in. cubes quickly. Using spoon, slather sweet potato pulp over tortillas; layer on onion, then shark. Fold classic style and serve immediately seam side down. If fish should cool, this dish can be easily microwaved in 1 minute.

Yield: 12 burritos

NOTE: A hearty side of red beans and rice Cajun style is good with this dish, or any other vegetable-rice pilaf.

Grilled Garlic
Scallop Burrito

▼ ▼ ▼

This is one of my absolute favorite burritos; a really scintillating indulgence for garlic lovers. Plan on an average of 4 fat scallops (1½– 2 in. in diameter) per burrito; if available scallops are smaller, simply use 5 to 6 per serving. Please watch these dainty morsels carefully as you're cooking them since they take very little time to brown and can burn easily if the grill rack is too close to the heating element. You may even wish to practice on an extra scallop prior to grilling the whole bunch.

▲ ▲ ▲

48 fresh scallops
Olive oil
½ cup butter
2 cloves garlic, crushed
½ tsp. salt
½ tsp. black pepper
12 whole wheat tortillas, warmed

½ cup 1-in. cubes sourdough bread, crusts removed
¼ cup chopped cilantro
1 medium tomato, diced, seeded, and drained
½ cup chopped raddichio
3 lemons, quartered
Tartar or seafood cocktail sauce (optional)

Preheat the broiler. Brush scallops with oil, place on broiler rack, and broil 3 minutes on each side. Watch carefully to see that scoremarks are brown, not black. Turn off broiler, cover scallops with sheet of foil to keep warm while fixing butter sauce. Melt the butter in a small saucepan over a medium heat. Add garlic, salt, and pepper, and increase heat to high for 1 minute, stirring constantly. Remove from heat and set aside. Remove scallops from broiler and portion 4 scallops per tortilla, placing them in a line down center of tortilla. Add bread pieces to garlic-butter sauce, stirring to make sure all pieces absorb equal amounts of liquid. Portion garlic-bread pieces, cilantro, tomato, and raddichio equally over scallops. Fold tortillas classic style and place seam side down on plate. Garnish each burrito with a lemon wedge and optional dollop of tartar or cocktail sauce. Serve immediately.

Yield: 12 burritos

Swordfish-Pesto Burrito

This recipe is perfect for those warm, starry summer nights. Just fire up the ol' barbeque grill and relax in a lawn chair. To lessen prep time, I suggest making the pesto in advance (omitting the cheese!), then freezing it until the night before you need it. Let it defrost slowly, add the cheese, and grind until paste is smooth. Do not refreeze. If you have some burritos left over, invite the neighborhood over, they'll love it . . . and you!

PESTO

4 oz. fresh basil leaves

½ cup grated Parmesan cheese

4 fresh spinach leaves

¾ cup grated Pecorino cheese

4 sprigs parsley

½ cup olive oil

3 sprigs marjoram

3 cloves garlic

BURRITOS

Two 1-lb. swordfish steaks

¼ cup pine nuts

12 blue corn tortillas, warmed

Pound all pesto ingredients in mortar using pestle or use food processor until all ingredients are reduced to a creamy paste. Set aside.

Fire up the barbeque grill using charcoal (and mesquite wood, if you can find it, for an additional smoky flavor). Wait for the coals to turn white. Place steaks on the grill and let cook until desired degree of doneness (fish should be firm, slightly moist, and have rich brown score marks from grill). Remove skin and cut fish into bite-size chunks. Place fish in large bowl and quickly mix in pesto and pine nuts. Spread tortillas on board and equally portion fish mixture on them. Fold using jelly roll method and place seam side down on plate; serve immediately. If burritos need to be warmed, wrap individually in foil and place on hot grill for a few minutes.

Yield: 12 burritos, 1½ cups pesto

Chinese Crab-Asparagus Burrito

Derived from a popular Chinese restaurant dish, this burrito is wrapped in rice paper like an egg roll. Since the recipe is a bit on the saucy side, make sure to use two layers of rice paper when wrapping your burrito.

One 12-oz. package frozen crab, thawed and drained

⅓ cup canned chicken broth

2 tsp. cornstarch

2 Tb. cooking sherry

1 tsp. soy sauce

1 tsp. sugar

¼ tsp. crushed red pepper flakes

2 Tb. sesame oil

1 tsp. grated fresh ginger root

1 cup 1-in. lengths asparagus

1 cup bean sprouts

¼ cup chopped green onions

20 sheets rice paper (egg roll skins)

Peanut oil (or corn or other oil)

Cut crab into bite-size pieces, set aside. In a medium bowl, stir broth into cornstarch; add sherry, soy sauce, sugar, and pepper flakes; mix, set aside. Pour sesame oil into preheated wok or skillet* over high heat. Add ginger and asparagus; stir-fry for 4 minutes, or until asparagus is slightly tender. Add crab, bean sprouts, and onions; stir-fry for 2 minutes. Slowly pour broth mixture into wok or skillet, stirring well. Continue to cook and stir until broth mixture thickens and begins to bubble; lower heat, cover wok or skillet, and simmer for 12 minutes, stirring occasionally.

On a board, separate rice paper leaves into 10 portions (2 squares per burrito). Spoon crab mixture onto center of rice paper leaves; fold pocket-square style. Moisten exposed edge and press down gently to seal seam. Clean skillet or wok and fill with peanut or corn oil to a

*If you have pet birds in your home, do not preheat nonstick skillets or electric woks. Most nonstick coatings emit odorless fumes that are fatal to birds within minutes of heating. Instead, pour oil into skillet first, then heat until oil sizzles when a drop of water is added. This recipe is just as delicious cooked in regular pans and woks.

depth of 1 inch. Place skillet over high heat or set wok thermostat at 350 degrees. When oil is hot (check with deep fat thermometer if necessary), place 1 or 2 burritos in oil. When egg roll skin begins to crisp and turn golden brown on bottom, turn burrito over. When both sides are browned, remove burrito and drain on paper towels. Repeat process until all burritos are fried.

Yield: 10 burritos

Chilled Summer Ceviche Burrito

▼ ▼ ▼

One of the few burritos designed to be served cold, its light refreshing flavor is perfect for midsummer dining. I sampled this delight at a takeout stand near the edge of a large olive grove about 3 miles south of Ensenada, Mexico, in 1980. The elderly proprietor nodded and smiled at me, his gold tooth sparkling in the sun, as I asked about the ingredients. Alas, he spoke no English and my Spanish was very rusty at the time, so this recipe is a best-guess duplication. When I returned the following summer, the stand had disappeared.

▲ ▲ ▲

½ lb. shrimp, cooked and deveined	1 large red tomato, diced
1 medium jicama	1 celery stalk, diced
2 medium avocados	6 large whole wheat tortillas, steamed and cooled
2 tsp. fresh lime juice	
6 Tb. mayonnaise	6 sprigs fresh cilantro
¼ tsp. chili powder	½ cup shredded raddichio

Remove tails from shrimp. Peel and dice jicama into small pieces. Peel, pit, and dice avocado into medium pieces. Place shrimp, jicama, and avocado in large mixing bowl, add lime juice, and stir well to prevent discoloration. In small bowl mix mayonnaise and chili powder until well blended. Add mayonnaise, tomato, and celery to shrimp mixture; mix well. Spread tortillas on board; place one sprig cilantro on each. Portion shrimp mixture and raddichio evenly on each tortilla. Fold burritos using classic method, place on cookie sheet, cover with plastic wrap, and refrigerate for at least 30 minutes. Remove from refrigerator, place on plates, and serve.

Yield: 6 burritos

VARIATIONS: Substitute ¼ cup chopped fresh mint leaves for cilantro. Substitute ½ cup grated coconut for raddichio, and add ½ cup pineapple chunks. Omit tomato.

Herbed Tuna Burrito

▼ ▼ ▼

This one's more fun than tuna helper and smells incredible. A friend and I were sifting through my collection of burrito recipes when she mentioned that there seemed to be a lack of fish-oriented fillings. I grimaced and suggested there was probably a good reason. My friend, never one to let a challenge go by untried, decided to experiment on her own and bring a sample to me for a taste test. The result follows.

▲ ▲ ▲

Two 6½-oz. cans white albacore tuna (packed in water)

1 red pepper, seeded and cut into thin strips

1 yellow pepper, seeded and cut into thin strips

8 flour tortillas, warmed

4 hard-boiled eggs, peeled and cooled

¾ cup mayonnaise

2 tsp. Dijon mustard

¼ tsp. black pepper

¼ tsp. paprika

1 Tb. dried capers

2 Tb. chopped fresh parsley

½ tsp. dried rosemary

½ tsp. dried tarragon

½ tsp. dried chervil

Drain tuna and break into small pieces in bowl. Divide equal amounts of tuna and red and yellow peppers among tortillas; do not fold! Chop eggs; in medium bowl combine eggs with mayonnaise, mustard, pepper, paprika, capers, parsley, rosemary, tarragon, and chervil. Mix well until smooth. Spoon half the egg mixture over tuna; reserve remainder. Fold filled tortillas using jelly roll method, and place seam side down in shallow baking dish. Spoon remaining egg mixture over burritos and place under broiler until bubbly. Serve immediately.

Yield: 8 burritos

Lobster and Rice Burrito

▼ ▼ ▼

I discovered this oddity in a sleepy little fishing town on the Pacific Coast, about 45 minutes south of Tijuana. "Town" may actually be a misnomer; each of the dozen or so wood clapboard houses turned out to be a restaurant! Even more strange, each restaurant served nothing but lobster dishes. As my companion and I walked from restaurant to restaurant, we noticed many net-heavy boats lined up on the beach or anchored near shore. After learning that the locals had a *prix fixe* on lobster (no friendly competition here), we picked an eatery at random and entered. Yelling to be heard over the extremely loud mariachi band, our waiter informed us that the entire citizenry was related by marriage and that each morning the men would check the lobster traps while the women prepared the day's rice and refried beans. Sometimes truth is stranger than fiction!

▲ ▲ ▲

2 small onions, chopped

4 Tb. canola oil, or unsaturated vegetable oil

1 green pepper, seeded and cut into thin strips

1 lb. raw lobster meat, shredded

¾ cup dry white wine

2½ cups canned chicken broth

1 cup Homemade Tomato Sauce (see page 128)

½ tsp. garlic powder

½ tsp. chili powder

½ tsp. salt

½ tsp. black pepper

2 cups cooked rice

6 blue corn tortillas

In a large skillet, sauté onions in oil until onions are translucent and soft. Add green pepper and lobster; cook until lobster takes on a reddish color. Add wine, chicken broth, tomato sauce, and seasonings. When mixture comes to a boil, add rice and stir well. Cover skillet and lower heat; simmer until liquid is absorbed, 40–50 minutes. Rice should be soft, but not mushy. Using a large spoon, place mixture on each tortilla along an imaginary center line. Wrap in classic style and serve immediately.

Yield: 6 burritos

BEEF

Cactus-Burger Burrito

The napilita cactus has a thin, broad, flat leaf that is used in many southwestern dishes or as an appetizer when broiled by itself. Sold in cans or fresh at specialty shops, it initially has the consistency and "mouth feel" of biting into a slice of cucumber with the skin left on. But as one chews, the formerly firm veggie turns slightly gelatinous and releases its uniquely distinctive flavor. I prefer cutting it into thin strips to facilitate cooking; this also reduces the mushiness.

6 napilita cactus leaves	1 cup bread crumbs
2 Tb. vegetable oil	2 eggs, beaten
2 medium onions, diced	12 blue corn tortillas, warmed
4 lbs. lean ground beef	1 cup shredded cheddar cheese
2 tsp. chili powder	1½ cup shredded mixed lettuces
½ cup finely chopped fresh cilantro	Ranchera Sauce (see page 124) (optional)
2 celery stalks, finely diced	
2 tsp. salt	

Preheat broiler. Wash cactus leaves well under cold water; pat dry and place on broiler rack. Slide rack into broiler, keeping a close eye to see that heat source does not wither or blacken cactus. Cactus leaves are done when edges are lightly browned but flat and leaf is still green and firm. Cut cooked cactus leaves into 1/4-in.-thick strips, wrap in foil to keep warm, and set aside.

Heat oil in large frying pan over medium-high heat; add onions and cook until soft and lightly golden. In a large mixing bowl, combine ground beef, chili powder, cilantro, celery, salt, bread crumbs, and eggs. Blend with hands until well mixed, then add to frying pan. Brown beef mixture, stirring frequently to avoid sticking or burning. Drain any excess oil before filling burritos.

Portion cactus strips equally among tortillas; top with ground beef mixture, cheese, and lettuce. Fold classic style and serve immediately, smothered with warmed ranchera sauce, if desired.

Yield: 12 burritos

Chilean Meat and Corn Burrito

▼ ▼ ▼

Pastel de Choclo is a prominent national dish from Chile; it is baked as a casserole with a topping of pureed corn. Several of my friends who've hiked in the Andes have sampled it, and each reports varying degrees of spicy heat. I've adapted the basic wholesomeness of this simple dish by adding whole, mild Anaheim green chilies and omitting the raisins, among other things. The result is a medium-hot burrito with a more substantial texture.

▲ ▲ ▲

2 Tb. vegetable oil	1 Tb. flour
2 medium onions, sliced and pushed into rings	1 lb. spicy chorizo sausage
1 clove garlic, crushed	1 cup sliced black olives
1 lb. lean ground beef	1 cup canned corn, drained
1 tsp. salt	12 canned roasted whole Anaheim chilies
1 tsp. cumin	12 corn tortillas, warmed
½ tsp. chili powder	Gila Bend Salsa Verde (see page 126) (optional)

Heat oil in large frying pan on medium-high heat; add onions and garlic and sauté until onions are soft. Add ground beef, salt, cumin, chili powder, and flour; stir frequently as ground beef browns. In separate pan, fry chorizo until brown; drain off grease (there will probably be plenty), then add chorizo, olives, and corn to ground beef mixture in large pan. Stir well to mix, then lower heat to medium and place whole chilies gently on top to warm 1–2 minutes. Remove pan from heat and place 1 chili on top of each tortilla. Portion meat-corn mixture among tortillas, roll classic style, and serve immediately. If desired, serve with small bowl of Gila Bend Salsa Verde, which can be spooned over the burritos for a fiery feast.

Yield: 12 burritos

Marinated Flank Steak Burritos

▼ ▼ ▼

An upscale version of the skirt steak burrito rolled with iceberg lettuce and tomato commonly found at Southern Californian taco stands. The idea is to capitalize on the contrast of temperatures: meat should be sizzling hot, while vegetables should be icy cold. Any kind of salsa is suitable for a room temperature "binder," but I prefer the unusual zest of the tomatillo. See recipe for Tomatillo Salsa on page 131, and make it before steaks are put onto grill. A lunchtime variation would feature all ingredients at room temperature; i.e., the equivalent of a haughty roast beef sandwich.

▲ ▲ ▲

2 **flank steaks (about 2 lbs. each)**

½ **cup soy sauce**

2 **Tb. garlic powder**

12 **corn tortillas, warmed**

1 **cup Tomatillo Salsa (see page 131)**

12 **sprigs fresh cilantro, chilled**

2 **cups shredded raddichio, chilled**

1 **cup shredded Havarti cheese, chilled**

Make latticework cuts on both sides of steaks with sharp knife, making sure not to cut all the way through meat. Brush soy sauce on both sides of each steak, making sure sauce is absorbed into each slice mark. Sprinkle tops of steaks with garlic powder and place on heated rack for grilling over coals, or place on broiler rack 3–4 in. away from heating element. Grill steaks to desired degree of doneness (medium-rare works best), turning meat over halfway through cooking time. Edges of meat should be seared while middle is pink and a bit juicy. Cut meat into thin strips and portion immediately onto tortillas; top with tomatilla salsa, cilantro, raddichio, and cheese. Roll classic style and serve immediately.

Yield: 12 burritos

VARIATION: Serve with a big bowl of Salsa Cruda, Santa Fe Guacamole (see recipes pages 132 and 128), and tortilla chips for a hearty, informal dinner or main-meal lunch.

Chilito Burrito

▼ ▼ ▼

A takeoff on the American "Sloppy Joe," this is an exceedingly messy burrito that should be eaten with a knife and fork. Should you wish to eat "hands on," just double the amount of fresh bread cubes as the sauce will soak into the bread and make the burrito much drier and easier to get a grip on. Tomatillos look like green tomatoes covered with a papery husk and can be found in most grocery stores nowadays. Peel off the husk and carefully scrub the tomato to remove all traces of slick, greasy residue before using.

▲ ▲ ▲

- 3 Tb. vegetable oil
- 2 cloves garlic, crushed
- 2 onions, finely diced
- 1 bell pepper, seeded and diced
- 2 tomatillos, diced
- 6 diced canned green chilies (mild Anaheim work best)
- 2 lbs. lean ground beef
- 14 oz. can peeled tomatoes
- 14 oz. can kidney beans
- 1 cup pitted and sliced black olives
- 4 Tb. brown sugar
- 2 tsp. chili powder
- 2 Tb. black pepper
- 2 tsp. salt
- 12 slices fresh bread, torn into small chunks
- 12 flour tortillas, warmed
- 1 cup grated cheddar cheese
- 1 cup grated Havarti cheese

Heat oil in large pot over medium-high heat; add garlic and onions. Cook until onions are soft and clear; lower heat slightly, and add bell pepper and tomatillos. Continue cooking until bell pepper pieces are just soft, stirring frequently. Add green chilies and ground beef. Brown the beef, stirring frequently. Add tomatoes with can juice, beans with can juice, olives, sugar, chili powder, black pepper, and salt. Stir well, then lower heat and simmer, covered, for 1½ hours. At 30-minute intervals, stir contents of pot to avoid sticking. Just before assembling burritos, stir in bread pieces gently. Allow bread to soak up as much chili juice as possible, then, using a slotted spoon, portion mixture among tortillas. Top with grated cheeses, fold classic style, and serve immediately.

Yield: 12 very messy burritos

Pepper Steak Burrito with Roquefort Garnish

▼ ▼ ▼

This exceptionally fine recipe was inspired by the equally fine preparation of pepper steak by Executive Chef Jerry Peters at the Enchantment Resort in Boynton Canyon, Arizona.

▲ ▲ ▲

10 Tb. plus 1 tsp. butter

3 Tb. sour cream

8 oz. Roquefort cheese

2 Tb. minced chives

2 cloves garlic, crushed

1 tsp. salt

2 Tb. steak sauce (A–1 is a good choice)

Two 12–14-oz. porterhouse steaks

4 Tb. black peppercorns

2 medium onions, sliced and pushed into rings

1 cup sliced mushrooms

½ cup red wine (cabernet sauvignon is good)

1 tsp. flour

12 flour tortillas, warmed

Combine 6 Tb. butter with next three ingredients in a small mixing bowl, beat with spoon until thoroughly blended; set aside. In another small mixing bowl, combine garlic, salt, and steak sauce. Brush one-half of sauce over tops of steaks. Sprinkle 2 Tb. peppercorns onto tops of steaks and press in firmly with fingers or mallet (use mallet gently or sauce will splatter). Turn steaks over and repeat process; meat should now be covered with sauce and peppercorns.

Melt 2 Tb. butter in a large frying pan over medium-high heat; add onions and mushrooms and fry until onions are golden brown. Using slotted spoon, remove onions and mushrooms and drain on paper towels; cover to keep warm.

Lower heat to medium and melt 2 Tb. butter; gently place steaks in pan so that peppercorns do not fall off and fry to desired degree of doneness (medium-rare works best). Remove steaks from pan and transfer to cutting board; sliver steaks and cover with foil to keep warm. Return onions and mushrooms to frying pan and add wine; turn up heat and boil 2—3 minutes, or until the mixture has reduced slightly. In small bowl, mash together remaining 1 tsp. butter with the flour, then add to frying pan, stirring constantly until it has been absorbed and sauce starts to thicken. Continue cooking 2—3 minutes, until sauce is thick.

Preheat oven to 350 degrees. Place steak slices on tortillas; using spoon, add onion-mushroom sauce. Fold classic style and place seam side down in baking dish. Dot each burrito with Roquefort cheese mixture and place in oven for 5 minutes, or until cheese mixture is slightly runny. Serve immediately.

Yield: 12 burritos

Polish Borscht Burrito

▼ ▼ ▼

A melting pot of colors, flavors, and textures, this surprisingly hearty meal starts off as meat loaf! Challenged to come up with a tasty alternative to leftover meat loaf smothered in tomato sauce, I adapted an inspired recipe from a Baltimore housewife acquaintance of Polish descent, then improvised until I achieved the following result. Of course, here we're making the meat loaf from scratch, but you can substitute any precooked meat loaf in equivalent amounts.

▲ ▲ ▲

MEAT LOAF

- ¼ cup unsalted butter
- 2 medium onions, thinly sliced and pushed into rings
- 2 cloves garlic, crushed
- 1½ lb. lean ground beef
- ½ lb. lean pork sausage
- 1½ cups seasoned bread crumbs
- 2 green onions, finely chopped
- 1 tsp. horseradish sauce (store-bought variety)
- 1 tsp. salt
- 1 tsp. black pepper
- ¼ tsp. dill
- ¼ tsp. oregano
- ¼ tsp. rosemary
- 1 large egg, lightly beaten
- ¼ cup sour cream

BURRITOS

- 3 carrots, julienned into 1-in. long strips
- 2 beets, julienned into 1-in. long strips
- 2 Tb. butter
- ½ cup sliced mushrooms
- Sour cream
- ⅛ tsp. black pepper
- ⅛ tsp. paprika
- 12 flour tortillas, warmed
- Wafer-thin beet curls

Preheat oven to 350 degrees.

Melt butter in medium frying pan over medium-high heat. Add onions and garlic and cook until onions are just golden brown. Pour mixture into a very large mixing bowl and let cool. Add other meat loaf ingredients with your hands, kneading well until all ingredients are blended. Spoon mixture into a 2-lb. loaf pan and smooth the top; cover with aluminum foil and bake 1–1¼ hours, or until a knife inserted in the center comes out clean. Remove from oven and cover.

Lightly steam carrot and beet strips until just tender; set aside and keep warm. Melt butter in medium saucepan over medium heat. Add mushrooms and cook until tender. Add 1½ cups sour cream, black pepper, and paprika, stirring constantly. Heat until sauce is smooth, about 5 minutes. Crumble warm meat loaf, then distribute evenly on top of tortillas. Add carrot and beet strips; top with enough sauce to just cover everything (do not smother). Roll tortillas classic style, place seam side down on plate, and garnish with a dollop of sour cream and a beet curl; serve immediately.

Yield: 12 burritos

Marinated Malay Burritos

▼ ▼ ▼

At a conference at the Rim Institute, high up in the pine-covered Mogollon Rim area of central Arizona, I met two fascinating people who were exchanging cook chores for workshop attendance. Leo and Raven had traveled extensively (even living with Huichol Indian shaman, Don José, in the Mexican wilderness for several summers!) and collected numerous mouth-watering recipes. The one described below is actually Asian in origin but easily adapts to Southwestern tastes.

▲ ▲ ▲

1 lb. stewing beef, cut into 1-in. cubes
½ cup plain yogurt
1 tsp. cayenne pepper
1 tsp. sea salt
1 tsp. dried coriander
½ tsp. ground ginger

½ cup brown rice
½ cup whole dried lentils
1 onion, thinly sliced
¼ cup vegetable oil
12 whole wheat tortillas, warmed

Combine meat with yogurt and spices and let marinate for several hours (2½ hours minimum, 3 hours is best). Boil 1 cup water in small pot; add rice, cover, and simmer for 40 minutes, or until rice has absorbed all the water. Boil 1½ cups water in another small pot; add lentils, cover, and simmer for 20 minutes, or until lentils are soft but not mushy. Put onion in large skillet and sauté in oil until golden brown about 5 minutes before lentils and rice are done. Add marinated beef mixture and simmer until meat is thoroughly cooked and sauce has thickened. To assemble burritos, spread tortillas on board. Layer equal portions of rice and lentils on each (no more than 2—3 teaspoons on each tortilla); using slotted spoon, add meat mixture to rice and lentils. Using pocket-square method, fold burritos carefully and place on plates, seam side down. Spoon sauce from beef mixture over each burrito and serve.

Yield: 12 burritos

VARIATION: Substitute lamb for beef.

Curried Burger Burritos

▼ ▼ ▼

Faced with a refrigerator filled with leftovers, I decided to experiment and test the results on some wary friends. Fortunately for me, it turned out great, and I had a new recipe. Again, this is one of those recipes where substitutions can often create new taste sensations. For authentic Indian flavor, substitute diced potatoes for tomatoes and add chutney. Pumpkin seeds (or *pepitos*) can replace sunflower seeds, while almost any grain can replace the wild rice.

▲ ▲ ▲

1 cup wild rice	4 oz. can tomato paste
1 medium yellow onion, chopped	1½ cups water
1 lb. ground beef	2 medium tomatoes, diced
1 Tb. vegetable oil	¼ cup raw sunflower seeds
3 tsp. curry powder	¼ cup peanuts, chopped
1 clove garlic, minced	Corn kernels from 1 fresh cob
½ tsp. cumin	8 large whole wheat tortillas, warmed

Rinse rice well. Boil, uncovered, in an unlimited amount of water until kernels have a nutlike flavor and chewy texture, about 1–1½ hours. Set aside.

Sauté onion and ground beef in oil until lightly browned. Drain and discard fat. Add curry powder, garlic, cumin, tomato paste, water, and tomatoes. Simmer 15 minutes, or until tomatoes are mushy. Add seeds, peanuts, and corn; simmer 5 minutes, then cover and turn off heat. Reheat rice (if prepared earlier and refrigerated) in oven or microwave. Spoon equal portions of rice and curried meat onto each tortilla. Use pocket-square fold and serve immediately.

Yield: 8 burritos

NOTE: An alternate method for preparing rice is to rinse rice well. Boil 3 cups of water in large pot; add rice. Lower heat, cover pot, and simmer for 1 hour. Rice will have a nutlike flavor and chewy texture.

VARIATION: Add 2 tsp. of Aged Baltimore Chutney to each burrito prior to folding.

Aged Baltimore Chutney

My roommate's mother recommends aging this chutney for at least a year but says it can be used as quickly as 3 months from sealing. Obviously, the longer it's sealed, the more integrated the flavors become.

8 cups diced tomatoes	5 cups chopped unpeeled apples
1 cup diced celery	
4 cups brown sugar, firmly packed	2 white onions, chopped
	4 cups vinegar
1 clove garlic, minced	1 tsp. ground ginger
2 tsp. allspice	2 tsp. mustard seed
½ tsp. cinnamon	1 tsp. white pepper

Combine all ingredients in a large pot. Heat slowly, stirring frequently, until sugar is completely dissolved. Continue simmering until mixture is thick and syrupy. Seal in heated, sterilized canning jars, and leave on a dark shelf for several months (the longer the better).

Yield: 4 two-pint jars of chutney

PORK

▼▼▼

Monte Cristo Burrito

▼▼▼

Over the last decade, you've seen it at Denney's, at Stuckey's, at any of a dozen nationwide restaurant chains that cater to travelers. It comes in a variety of sizes and disguises. It's got as many names as there are states in the union. But I know it as the Monte Cristo sandwich. You know—it's the specially priced combo of chicken (or turkey), ham, and cheese (cheddar, American, Swiss) on toasted bread (or coated in batter and deep-fried, or placed in a crêpe and smothered with more cheddar, American, or Swiss), and served with hash browns (or fries, or chips, or?). And we all have to admit secretly that while the Monte Cristo may not be glamorous, it is satisfying. There's something so homey about this homely dish that we forgive its fat content, its cholesterol count, its nineties naughtiness, and we eat millions of them every year! So close the curtains and lock the door . . . and enjoy this travel treat in the privacy of your own home . . . just don't tell the neighbors!

▲▲▲

- 2 Tb. butter
- 4 oz. cooked leftover chicken breast, shredded
- 4 oz. cooked Virginia or honey-baked ham, diced
- ½ small bell pepper, cut into thin strips
- ¼ tsp. salt
- ¼ tsp. black pepper
- ½ cup grated Gruyère cheese
- ¼ cup grated Havarti cheese
- 12 flour tortillas, warmed
- ¼ cup chopped parsley
- 2 hard-boiled eggs, sliced
- ¼ cup pitted and sliced black olives

Melt butter over medium-high heat; when frothy add chicken, ham, bell pepper, salt, and pepper. Stir until bell pepper is soft and chicken and ham are heated through. Lower heat slightly and add cheeses; stir until mixture is melted and coating other ingredients. Using a large spoon, portion the gooey mess equally on the tortillas; roll classic style and serve seam side down on plate. Sprinkle parsley over top of tortillas, place egg slices artistically (usually 2 or 3 to each burrito), and add olives.

Yield: 12 burritos

NOTE: If chicken and ham absorb the butter and cheese is too thick, add another teaspoon of butter until cheese has a runny consistency. Make sure to keep heat low enough so cheese does not brown or crisp.

Kidney Bean–Chorizo Burrito

▼▼▼

Not for the faint-hearted nor those who are watching their cholesterol count, this extra-hot recipe comes straight from a greasy spoon in south Texas. The place had one enormously fat, scraggly bearded, non-English-speaking cook; three walls made of corrugated aluminum rescued from a condemned building (the condemned sign still attached, thank you very much); and no sign announcing this fine establishment's nom de business. It also had ridiculously long lines (more than three men waiting is considered unbelieveable in most places like this . . . and women are never visible), a sure indication of something good afoot. After elbowing my way through the slurping and scarfing crowd of burly bruisers, I managed to order (pointing in the general direction of the hand-scrawled menu written on sheets of loose-leaf) and received what is re-created below. I'm still not sure if it was a joke or not. I do know that the chorizo sausages were homemade, and that I needed three Cokes to quench the fire! Maybe the conspicuously absent women knew something I didn't!

▲ ▲ ▲

12 medium-size extra-spicy chorizo sausages, skinned and cut into 1-inch-long pieces

Vegetable shortening or lard

2 large onions, diced

2 large beefsteak tomatoes, seeded, diced, and drained

4 jalapeño peppers, finely diced, not seeded, or ¼ cup sliced bottled jalapeño peppers

1 tsp. black pepper

½–1 tsp. cayenne pepper (depending on whether or not you want to keep your tastebuds intact)

2 cups cooked kidney beans drained and mashed

1 cup grated jack cheese

½ cup sliced black olives

12 large corn tortillas, warmed

Fry chorizo pieces in medium-size pan over medium heat 5–6 minutes, stirring occasionally; chances are they will let out a lot of grease. Remove chorizo when just browned and drain on paper towels. Measure chorizo grease; add enough vegetable shortening or lard to make 3 Tb. and reserve. Discard remaining chorizo grease, if any, and wipe pan clean with paper towel. Place the 3 Tb. fat in pan over medium-high heat; add onions and fry until golden, but don't brown. Stir in tomatoes, jalapeños, pepper, and chili powder; cook 5–6 minutes, or until tomato starts to soften, stirring frequently. Stir in chorizo, beans, cheese, and olives. Cook, stirring frequently (remember to lift from bottom to keep beans and cheese from sticking), for 10 minutes. Spoon mixture onto tortillas, roll classic style, and serve immediately.

Yield: 12 burritos

VARIATIONS: Garnish with shredded lettuce, diced tomato, grated cheese, sour cream, and top with a black olive; or smother in a chunky ranchero sauce.

Hazelnut-Pork Burrito

The technical assistant at Columbia College in Hollywood was a young Libyan man whose family had forced him to emigrate after sensing the trouble that was about to descend on that desert land. He made it out just in time; the borders were closed two weeks later. Mohammed collected antique film cameras and loved to astound visitors with ancient reels of stock movie footage while serving the most wonderful all-in-one dishes from the culinary heritage of his homeland. I can still remember laughing with friends while Mo shared these turn-of-the-century flicks and wonderful food with us. It was definitely ''a Kodak moment'' in real life.

4 Tb. peanut oil

1 clove garlic, crushed

1 large onion, sliced and pushed into rings

4 lbs. pork or lamb, cut into 1-in. cubes

2 tsp. salt

2 tsp. black pepper

1 cup raw peanut pieces, crushed almost into powder

4 Tb. soy sauce

1 tsp. chili powder

1 lb. red seedless grapes (Red Flame variety preferred)

1 cup dry-roasted peanut halves

12 flour tortillas, warmed

½ cup finely chopped fresh parsley

2 medium tomatoes, seeded and diced

Heat peanut oil in large frying pan over medium-high heat; add garlic and onion. Cook onion until soft, then add pork, salt, and pepper. Stirring frequently, brown pork well (about 10 minutes). Add crushed peanuts, soy sauce, and chili powder; stir well until all ingredients are blended. Lightly stir in grapes and lower heat, simmering 10–15 minutes, or until pork is very tender. Lightly stir in peanut halves and continue simmering for 1 minute, stirring frequently. Spoon mixture onto tortillas, top with parsley and tomatoes; fold classic style and serve immediately.

Yield: 12 burritos

Ham and Mushroom Burrito

These finger-size burritos are perfect as a hot appetizer at parties since they are rolled thin and are rather inexpensive to make.

¼ cup butter

2 medium onions, sliced and pushed into rings

2 cloves garlic, crushed

2 tsp. black pepper

½ cup shelled raw sunflower seeds

2 cups honey-baked ham, cut into thin strips

2 cups straw mushrooms

2 Tb. apricot preserves

12 flour tortillas, warmed

Melt butter in large frying pan over medium-high heat; add onions, garlic, pepper, and sunflower seeds. Cook, stirring constantly, until seeds are just starting to brown. Lower heat and add ham; cook for 3 minutes, stirring frequently (make sure to lift seeds so they don't stick to bottom of pan). Add mushrooms; continue cooking for 2 minutes, stirring gently. Add preserves and stir gently, letting mixture thicken for 2 minutes. Remove from heat; portion onto tortillas and roll thinly in classic style.

Yield: 12 burritos

Italian Sausage Burrito

▼ ▼ ▼

When most people think of hominy, they think of grits; however, either yellow or white whole-kernel hominy has a firm texture and slightly sweet taste that perfectly complements the gentle anise undertone of authentic Italian sausages. Great Northern beans add bulk and nutrition without much conflict in taste, so they are a perfect extender; these beans also readily absorb the seasoned tomato sauce and help convey the entire taste of this welcome winter dish.

▲ ▲ ▲

1 Tb. olive oil	½ tsp. black pepper
1½ lb. Italian sausages	2 tsp. sugar
2 cloves garlic, crushed	4 whole canned Anaheim mild green chilies
2 small onions, sliced and pushed into rings	1 cup hominy, cooked (not hominy grits, but the whole kernel)
14 oz. can Italian plum tomatoes, with juice	1 cup cooked Great Northern beans
1 tsp. sage	12 flour tortillas, warmed
1 tsp. oregano	

Heat oil in large frying pan over medium-high heat; add sausages and brown. Remove sausages and drain them on paper towels; cut into bite-size pieces. Fry garlic and onion in sausage grease until onion is golden brown. Drain off all but 2 Tb. of sausage grease. Add tomatoes with can juice and bring to a boil, stirring occasionally; add sage, oregano, pepper, and sugar, and stir again. Add sausage to pan; add chilies, hominy, and beans. Lower heat to medium and cook 10–12 minutes, stirring frequently (liquid should reduce greatly). When mixture is fairly dry, remove pan from heat and portion mixture equally among tortillas; fold classic style and serve immediately.

Yield: 12 burritos

VARIATION: Garnish top of burrito generously with freshly made Salsa Cruda (see page 132).

Vindaloo Pork Burrito

▼ ▼ ▼

I've updated the traditional Indian curry dish into a saucy-style burrito with a tangy-sweet surprise: slices of mandarin orange inside! For more "bite," substitute an equal amount of seeded tangerine slices. Note that an electric blender is necessary here and that the marinated pork is made up the day before.

▲ ▲ ▲

2 Tb. grated fresh ginger

4 cloves garlic, crushed

1 tsp. chili powder

2 tsp. turmeric

2 tsp. salt

6 whole cloves

6 whole peppercorns

½ tsp. cinnamon

1 Tb. coriander seed

1 Tb. cumin seed

¾ cup white wine vinegar

2 lb. pork fillets or tenderloin, cut into 1-in. cubes

2 Tb. butter

1 large onion, sliced and pushed into rings

2 carrots, thinly sliced

2 potatoes, cut into 1-in. cubes

½ cup water

12 whole wheat tortillas

60 mandarin orange slices (8 oranges separated into 8 sections each)

12 sprigs fresh cilantro

Put first eleven ingredients into an electric blender and blend on high speed for 30 seconds, or until mixture forms a smooth paste. Put pork in a large mixing bowl and stir in the spice paste; cover bowl and let marinate at room temperature for at least 1 hour (no more than 1½ hours). Stir mixture once, making sure all sides of pork are coated. Place in refrigerator overnight. An hour before cooking time, remove pork from fridge and uncover; let sit. Heat butter in a large frying pan over medium-high heat; add onion and fry until golden brown. Lower heat to medium and add carrot, potatoes, water, and marinated pork (scrape all paste from bowl into pan). Stir well, then increase heat until mixture is boiling. Cover pan, reduce heat to low, and simmer for 30 minutes. Uncover, stir gently, replace cover, and continue cooking for another 20–30 minutes, or until pork is very tender and sauce is rather thick. (You can add a bit of flour to thicken sauce if necessary). Using a slotted spoon, portion curry onto tortillas. Top curry with 4 mandarin orange slices per burrito, roll up in classic style, and place seam side down on plates. Drizzle remaining sauce over top of burritos and garnish with a sprig of cilantro and another mandarin orange slice.

Yield: 12 burritos

Marinated Asian Pork Burrito

▼ ▼ ▼

I love all sorts of Asian food. The Pearl restaurant, a tiny eatery specializing in Vietnamese cuisine in midtown Los Angeles, serves up sizzling pork loin with a distinctly Japanese undertone. The cook does not speak much English, but I managed to learn a few ingredients of his superior marinade; the rest I ferreted out through trial and error. The results, and a truly toothsome burrito, await you.

▲ ▲ ▲

½ cup soy sauce	4 Tb. sesame oil
⅛ cup rice wine	1 cup straw mushrooms
¼ cup water	½ cup carrots, grated into 1-in. strips
4 Tb. sugar	
2 cloves garlic, crushed	2 cups bean sprouts
1 Tb. grated fresh ginger	1 cup plum sauce or sweet-and-sour sauce
1 tsp. black pepper	
3 lb. pork fillets	12 large flour tortillas, warmed

In a large mixing bowl, combine first seven ingredients. Add pork fillets one by one, turning to make sure all meat surfaces have been coated in marinade. Cover bowl and let sit at room temperature for 3 hours; rearrange meat every 30 minutes so that all sides are evenly coated.

Preheat oven to 350 degrees. Coat inside of large baking dish evenly with 2 Tb. sesame oil; remove pork fillets from marinade and arrange in baking dish. Cook in preheated oven 50–60 minutes, or until pork is tender. Turn off heat and leave pan in oven to keep warm. Heat 2 Tb. sesame oil in wok or large frying pan; when oil sizzles, add mushrooms, carrot, and bean sprouts. Fry for 3 minutes, stirring constantly; bean sprouts should just begin to turn soft. Cover wok or pan, turn off heat, and keep vegetables warm. Smear tortillas with plum or sweet-and-sour sauce, leaving a 1-inch border around edges. Remove pork from oven, quickly cut into long thin strips and portion evenly among tortillas. Top with stir-fried vegetables, roll classic style, and serve immediately.

Yield: 12 tortillas

Knockwurst-Pepper Burrito

Regular hot dogs, bratwurst, or other type precooked meat sausage can be substituted for knockwurst, depending on taste.

2 Tb. vegetable oil	1 tsp. black pepper
1 large yellow onion, chopped	1 tsp. chili powder
1 clove garlic, chopped	1 tsp. paprika
1 large green bell pepper, seeded and cut into thin strips	1 tsp. Mrs. Dash spicy variety
1 large red bell pepper, seeded and cut into thin strips	12 knockwurst or frankfurters
14 oz. can peeled tomatoes, with juice	12 whole wheat tortillas, warmed
	6 oz. can tomato sauce (optional)

Heat oil over medium-high heat in large frying pan. Add onion and garlic and fry for about 8 minutes, or until onion is golden brown. Add green and red pepper, continue frying, stirring constantly, for 6 minutes. Add tomatoes with juice, pepper, chili powder, paprika, and Mrs. Dash seasoning. Reduce heat to low, cover pan, and simmer for 30 minutes, stirring occasionally. Cut knockwurst into pieces 1 in. long; add to pan, stir, cover, and continue simmering for 15 minutes. Using slotted spoon, fill each tortilla with knockwurst-pepper mixture, fold pocket-square style, and serve seam side down. For moist version, place burritos in casserole dish, cover with remaining sauce, and bake in preheated 350-degree oven for 10 minutes. If there isn't enough sauce, add the optional tomato sauce to make necessary amount.

Yield: 12 burritos

Quick Ham-and-Rice Burrito

▼ ▼ ▼

What to do when you've come home late from work and your loved ones are expecting a hot meal? Maximize your time by using readily available or instant ingredients. There are several varieties of instant rice (including brown) on the market now; canned ham (or even sandwich slices) is usually in everybody's refrigerator; canned vegetables (drained, then rinsed well) are acceptable in a pinch too. Simply combine, add a bit of salsa or sauce, and serve. Voilà!

▲ ▲ ▲

1½ cups cooked brown and wild rice pilaf

1 Tb. butter

2 eggs, lightly beaten

2 Tb. vegetable, peanut, or sesame oil

1 lb. fresh green beans, blanched and cut into 1-in. pieces

2 lb. cooked ham, cut into 1-in. cubes

6 green onions, chopped

1 cup chopped cilantro

Salt and pepper to taste

12 whole wheat tortillas, warmed

Melt butter in a large frying pan over medium heat; add eggs and lightly scramble. Remove eggs from pan, break into bits with fingers and reserve. Heat oil in same pan over medium-high heat; add rice, beans, ham, and onions. Cook for 4 minutes, stirring constantly so rice doesn't stick and everything is heated through (beans will remain somewhat crisp). Reduce heat to medium-low, and add cilantro and egg pieces, stirring constantly. Cook 2–3 minutes, or until everything is piping hot; add salt and pepper to taste. Spoon onto whole wheat tortillas, fold classic style, and serve immediately.

Yield: 12 burritos

VARIATION: Stir in 4 Tb. mustard or 4 Tb. sweet-and-sour sauce prior to filling tortillas for added zest.

Hot Dog Burritos

▼ ▼ ▼

This fanciful take on the American ballpark delight will charm children of all ages.

▲ ▲ ▲

12 frankfurters

12 flour tortillas, warmed

Mustard

Pickle relish

12 strips lean bacon, cooked, drained, and patted dry

1½ cups grated cheddar cheese

6 green onions, chopped

2 medium tomatoes, diced

Drop frankfurters into boiling water (or beer, for adults) and cook for 5 minutes, then simmer over medium heat for 10 minutes. Spread top side of tortillas with mustard and pickle relish. Lay one strip of bacon down center of each "dressed" tortilla; sprinkle on cheddar cheese, onions, and tomatoes. Remove frankfurters from water (or beer), drain. Place one hot dog in center of each filled burrito, roll classic style, and serve immediately.

Yield: 12 burritos

Brunch Burrito

Simple and quick, this recipe can easily be doubled to accommodate unexpected guests. Variations can be created with the addition of grated cheddar, ripe avocado slices, even corn and adzuki beans!

- 6 slices bacon
- 1 medium onion, thinly sliced
- 3 medium tomatoes, diced
- 6 eggs
- 1 cup sour cream
- ½ cup chopped fresh parsley
- 1 tsp. dry mustard
- ¼ tsp. dill
- ¼ tsp. cayenne pepper
- ¼ tsp. marjoram
- 6 whole wheat tortillas, warmed
- 6 sprigs fresh parsley (optional)
- 6 tsp. caviar (optional)

Fry bacon crisp; remove from pan, blot with paper towels, and crumble. Discard all but 2 Tb. bacon drippings; sauté onion and tomatoes until soft. Add eggs, ½ cup sour cream, and seasonings, and scramble over low heat until desired degree of doneness is reached. Portion egg mixture evenly on tortillas; use classic-style fold. Garnish each burrito with a sprig of parsley, a dollop of sour cream, and caviar, if desired.

Yield: 6 burritos

South-of-the-Border
Eggs Benedict Burrito

My friends are crazy about this one. Chorizo is now being stocked regularly in most supermarkets. If your local store doesn't carry it, try going to a specialty or gourmet shop. Spicy Italian sausages can also be substituted for a different effect.

SAUCE

4 egg yolks	1 Tb. lemon juice
¼ tsp. salt	½ cup butter
½ tsp. dry mustard	

BURRITOS

1 lb. ground chorizo (spicy Mexican sausage)	8 flour tortillas, warmed
8 eggs	½ cup sliced black olives (optional)

Put yolks, salt, mustard, and lemon juice in blender jar. Cover and blend on low until well mixed. Heat butter in small pan until melted, then immediately pour into blender jar. Keep blender speed on low until mixture thickens. To keep sauce warm while making burritos, pour mixture into a double boiler and keep over hot, but not boiling, water until ready to use, remembering to stir occasionally.

Place chorizo in skillet and fry until well browned; drain excess fat and blot chorizo with paper towels, if necessary, to eliminate excess grease. Poach eggs to desired degree of doneness. Place 1 poached egg in the middle of each tortilla; top with chorizo. Fold pocket-square style, and spoon sauce over each burrito; garnish with olives, if desired. Serve hot.

Yield: 8 burritos, with ¾ cup sauce

LAMB

▼ ▼ ▼

Lamb-Artichoke Burrito

▼ ▼ ▼

This rather simple recipe is easy to fix in less than 30 minutes, and even easier to stretch with the addition of more rice in case the boss comes over unexpectedly. While lamb and artichokes are considered upscale ingredients, it is the touch of wine that unites the disparate flavors and textures in a creamy sauce. To also cut time, you can combine the 4 tsp. butter and flour before adding to pan; this helps in their easy absorption into the sauce.

▲ ▲ ▲

½ cup plus 4 tsp. butter

4 lbs. boned leg of lamb, cut into 1-in. cubes

2 tsp. salt

2 tsp. white pepper

1¼ cups dry white wine

48 canned artichoke hearts, diced
(about four 10-oz. cans)

2 cups peas

4 tsp. flour

1¼ cups heavy cream

12 flour tortillas, warmed

Melt ½ cup butter in large frying pan over medium-high heat; add lamb cubes, salt, and pepper, and brown, stirring frequently (should take 15–20 minutes at most). Transfer lamb to warmed ovenproof dish using slotted spoon; cover and keep warm. Pour the wine into the pan and stir constantly until mixture boils. Add artichoke hearts, peas, 4 tsp.

butter, and flour; stir constantly until sauce is smooth and thick. Lower heat slightly, add cream, and stir constantly until sauce is thoroughly heated, but not boiling. Remove pan from heat and cover. Portion lamb on tortillas; spoon on artichoke-pea mixture, making sure each burrito gets enough sauce to thoroughly wet ingredients. Fold tortillas in classic style and serve seam side down. Drizzle any remaining sauce over tops of burritos and serve immediately.

Yield: 12 burritos

Dill Lamb Burrito

▼ ▼ ▼

While not used extensively in the Southwestern states, dill is a regular ingredient in many Middle Eastern recipes. Of course, fresh dill (now commonly available at larger supermarkets) is preferably, but dry can also be used. If using fresh herb, halve the amount given in the recipe as it's twice as potent! A bit of cinnamon adds an unusual undertone to this intriguing dish.

▲ ▲ ▲

6 Tb. vegetable oil	2 tsp. black pepper
4 lb. leg of lamb, cut into 1-in. cubes	4 Tb. dried dill
3 onions, sliced and pushed into rings	1½ cups Frijoles Negros, warm (see page 139)
1 tsp. salt	12 whole wheat tortillas, warm
1 tsp. cinnamon	1 cup cooked pearl barley

Heat oil in large frying pan over medium-high heat; add lamb and brown for 10 minutes, stirring frequently. Add onions, salt, cinnamon, pepper, and dill; continue cooking, stirring occasionally, until lamb is thoroughly done (only the barest hint of pink in the middle). Cover pan and remove from heat. Spread beans over tortillas, top with barley grains. Portion seasoned lamb cubes on each tortilla using a slotted spoon. Fold in classic style and serve immediately.

Yield: 12 burritos

To-Kill-Ya Lamb Burrito

▼ ▼ ▼

Obviously this burrito recipe is not fatal or this book would not be in your hot little hands right now. It's a common joke among the young and bored on the border to order tequila affectionately as "to-kill-ya" ...all obvious inferences apply. And don't ask me...just picture all those sweet young faces plopping gracefully into their bowls of albondigas soup after one too many margaritas and you'll know where the phrase comes from, okay?

▲ ▲ ▲

1 cup tequila

1 large potato, cut into 1-in. cubes

1 carrot, cut into ¼-in. slices

1 crookneck squash, cut into ¼-in. slices

1 small zucchini, cut into ¼-in. slices

4 Tb. vegetable oil

1 lb. boned lamb, cut into 1-in. cubes

1 medium onion, sliced and pushed into rings

½ tsp. salt

½ tsp. black pepper

2 Tb. flour

12 large whole wheat tortillas, warmed

Put tequila in large bowl; add vegetables and marinate for 3 hours, stirring occasionally. Pour off tequila and drain veggies well, then let sit on paper towels. Heat oil in large frying pan over medium-high heat. Add lamb and fry until brown, stirring frequently. Add onion and continue frying for 3 minutes, stirring frequently until rings are soft and translucent. Mix salt and pepper with flour; add seasoned flour to pan a little at a time, stirring constantly. Add water until a thick gravy has formed (usually about 1 cup). If gravy is too thick or clumpy, add water 1 teaspoonful at a time. Turn up heat until gravy comes to a boil; add vegetables, lower heat, cover the pan, and simmer for at least 1 hour, or until meat is tender. Using a slotted spoon, portion all ingredients equally on tortillas; fold using classic style and place seam side down on plate. Smother burritos with remaining gravy and serve.

Yield: 12 hearty burritos

Marrakech Burrito

▼ ▼ ▼

An author friend of mine took a side trip to Morocco in 1989 and was swept away by the exotic and "terribly romantic" nature of the place. She brought back numerous amber necklaces, little bottles filled with musk incense pebbles, heavy belts made from old saddle leather, and this recipe. Of course, the Moroccans use unleavened flat bread as a scoop instead of tortillas, but the romance is intact. Play this one again and again, Sam!

▲ ▲ ▲

2 lbs. stewing lamb, cut into 1-in. cubes

¼ cup vegetable oil

2 medium yellow onions, chopped

3 medium tomatoes, chopped

½ cup coarsely chopped fresh parsley

½ tsp. salt

¼ tsp. turmeric

½ tsp. ground ginger

½ tsp. ground cinnamon

½ tsp. black pepper

12 oz. can artichoke hearts (packed in water, not marinated)

12 large whole wheat tortillas, warmed

In a large stew pot, sauté lamb in oil, making sure to stir cubes so all sides are browned equally. Add onions, and continue cooking until onions are golden. Reduce heat to low and mix in tomatoes, parsley, and seasonings. Simmer for 10 minutes. Rinse and drain artichoke hearts, cut into quarters, then add them to the pot. Continue simmering for another 10 minutes, stirring occasionally to make sure nothing sticks to the bottom of the pot. Spread tortillas on board. Using a slotted spoon (to rid filling of excess oil), equally portion mixture among tortillas. Use either classic fold or pocket-square fold and serve immediately.

Yield: 12 burritos

VEGETARIAN

▼ ▼ ▼

Smothered Anasazi-Tofu Burrito

▼ ▼ ▼

*A*nasazi is a Navajo word meaning "the ancient ones" and refers to a culture of Native Americans who built fabulous dwellings and ceremonial sites throughout the southwestern states. The Navajos believe that the Anasazi people were their ancestors, but since the Anasazi did not keep written records, very little is actually known about them. Beans excavated from Anasazi sites are still grown throughout Arizona and New Mexico today; the small rust and white beans have a taste and texture similar to the more common pinto bean.

▲ ▲ ▲

1 cup cooked Anasazi beans, drained

1 cup cooked quinoa, drained

½ cup firm tofu, well drained and crumbled

½ cup thinly sliced mushrooms

½ cup diced bell pepper

¼ cup chopped cilantro

1 cup chunky salsa (bought or homemade)

12 blue corn tortillas, warmed

2 cups grated soy cheese

1¼ cups enchilada sauce (bought or homemade)

24 black olives, sliced

Preheat oven to 300 degrees.

Lightly mix first six ingredients in large bowl with salsa; portion evenly on tortillas, top with 1 cup of the cheese and roll jelly-roll style. Place stuffed burritos in deep baking pan and pour over enchilada sauce; bake for 30 minutes. Remove from oven, sprinkle on remaining soy cheese and olives, and return to oven for another 5 minutes, or until cheese is melted. Serve immediately.

Yield: 12 burritos

Yogi Breakfast Burrito

A globe-trotting friend of mine who has spent considerable time in India and Nepal, living in ashrams and visiting various monasteries, told me of some saffron-robed disciples who regularly awaken at 4:00 A.M., perform an hour of silent meditation and prayer, then join with temple visitors for 2 hours of the most strenuous yoga exercises he'd ever seen. The kicker is that the monks would perform their physical rituals barefoot, in the snow, wearing only the simplest of loincloths. When my friend inquired about what kept the yogis from freezing during the often harsh winter months, he was told prana, or divine fire that burns within. He then laughingly told me of how he experienced this same prana without the rigorous exertion—he simply had breakfast with one of the local village families. Huge piles of spicy chilies, pungent peppers, and mustard were only the start, and the following recipe is an American adaptation of this fiery early-morning feast.

3 Tb. butter

1 large red onion, diced

2 Tb. freshly grated gingerroot

2 green Serrano chilies, diced, with seeds left intact

2 jalapeño chilies, diced, with seeds removed

½ tsp. turmeric (or 1 pinch saffron, if you can get it)

⅛ tsp. dry mustard

⅛ tsp. chili powder

¼ cup milk

8 eggs

1 medium tomato, diced

½ cup chopped fresh cilantro

12 corn tortillas, warmed

In a large frying pan, melt the butter over medium heat; add onion and fry until soft and translucent. Add ginger, chilies, turmeric, mustard, and chili powder, and fry for 1 minute, stirring constantly to keep chilies from burning. Lower heat slightly; whip milk and eggs together with whisk, then pour into pan. Scramble the eggs with onion-chili mixture for 1 minute, then add tomato and cilantro. Continue stirring until eggs are fluffy and slightly moist. Spoon mixture onto warm tortillas, fold pocket-square style, and serve immediately.

Yield: 12 burritos

Lentil Loaf Burrito

This recipe is an especially hearty one created for vegans (people who do not eat any animal products such as eggs, milk, cheese, etc.). Part of the recipe is derived from an Arrowhead Mills recipe and that has met with considerable approval from many of my vegetarian dinner guests.

2 cups cooked lentils

1 cup cooked brown rice

1 cup cooked bulgur

1 cup garbanzo flour mixed with ⅔ cup cold water

½ cup chopped walnuts

1 Tb. soy sauce

1 tsp. salt

1 tsp. sage

1 Tb. vegetable oil

18 whole wheat tortillas, warmed

1 cup very chunky salsa (bought or homemade)

1 cup grated soy cheese

1 cup shredded lettuce

1 cup shredded watercress

1 cup guacamole

18 whole black olives

Preheat oven to 350 degrees.

Drain the cooked lentils and grains well; in large bowl mix lentils, grains, flour mixture, nuts, soy sauce, salt, sage, and oil. Spoon into loaf pan and bake 30–45 minutes. Remove from oven and let set until firm, about 5 minutes. Break up loaf into bite-size crumbles and portion evenly on tortillas. Spoon salsa over loaf crumbles, then layer cheese, lettuce, and watercress on top. Fold filled tortillas in classic style and serve seam side down. Garnish each burrito with a teaspoonful of guacamole and a black olive.

Yield: 18 burritos

Ratty with Egg Burrito

▼ ▼ ▼

A takeoff on ratatouille with a funny name so children (and some grown men I know) will finally eat their veggies with gusto. This is also a healthy, tasty meal for vegetarians.

▲ ▲ ▲

1 medium eggplant
(about 2 lb.),
cut into finger-size sticks

2 medium zucchini
(about 1 lb.),
cut into ¼-in.-thick slices

2 tsp. salt

¼ cup olive or other
vegetable oil

1 large red onion, sliced into
rings

1 yellow bell pepper, seeded
and sliced into thin strips

1 cup sliced fresh
mushrooms

3 large tomatoes, diced

¼ tsp. garlic powder

¼ tsp. black pepper

⅛ tsp. thyme

⅛ tsp. basil

1 cup brown rice

2 Tb. butter

6 eggs, scrambled

12 whole wheat tortillas,
warmed

Very lightly sprinkle the eggplant and zucchini slices front and back with salt; place in collander and let drain for 30 minutes (this will eliminate excess moisture). Do not rinse; instead use paper towels to pat the pieces dry while heating the oil in large saucepan over medium-high heat. When oil sputters, add the onion and fry it until soft, 4–5 minutes. Add the eggplant and zucchini and cook for 10 minutes; if eggplant is turning brown too quick, lower heat and stir. Add pepper strips, mushrooms, tomatoes, and seasonings, and cook for 3 minutes, stirring occasionally. Loosely cover pan, lower heat, and simmer 40–45 minutes, making sure to stir occasionally. In pot, cook rice according to directions (usually brown rice takes about 40 minutes to absorb water added). About 5 minutes before the vegetable filling and rice are ready, melt butter in a separate frying pan and scramble the eggs until dry and fluffy. Arrange warmed tortillas on plate and assemble as follows: Using a spoon, portion eggs evenly in a line down middle of each tortilla; top egg with equal amount of rice; then using slotted ladle, spoon vegetable filling onto eggs and rice. Fold tortillas in classic style and serve seam side down. Any extra rice or filling can be combined and refrigerated or frozen for another meal.

Yield: 12 hearty burritos

VARIATION: Garnish each burrito with two splashes of Tabasco sauce, 1 Tb. grated sharp cheddar, 1 tsp. sour cream, and some sliced black olives. Olé!

Everything-but-the-Kitchen-Sink Burrito

▼ ▼ ▼

I know, I know, the list of ingredients sounds horrible, but it works. How do I know? A Nigerian classmate of mine played Florence Nightingale one evening when I was suffering from the flu prior to finals week. She pooh-poohed my request for chicken soup and scoured my (admittedly meager) supplies to make me something to "really get back on my feet." After our test frenzy, I asked her about the recipe. She laughed and said it was her mother's: "Anything on hand, including the kitchen sink." The ingredients below capture the essence of this glad-hand dish.

▲ ▲ ▲

4 green onions, chopped	1 lb. fresh spinach
½ yellow bell pepper, chopped	Chopped fresh mint (optional)
1 medium zucchini, chopped	½ tsp. black pepper
1 crookneck squash, chopped	1 tsp. garlic salt
1 Tb. vegetable oil	5 Tb. peanut butter
12 cherry tomatoes, halved	4 large flour tortillas
	Fresh mint sprigs (optional)

In large skillet, sauté onions, pepper, zucchini, and squash in oil until onions are golden. Add tomatoes, spinach, optional chopped mint, pepper, and garlic salt; continue to sauté, stirring frequently. Lower heat to a simmer; thin peanut butter with 3 or 4 Tb. warm water (add water a tablespoon at a time until the peanut butter becomes a thin paste), add to skillet and stir well. Continue to simmer for another 8–10 minutes, stirring frequently to prevent sticking or burning; remove from heat. Spread tortillas on board; portion filling equally among them, and fold burritos in the classic style. If desired, garnish with mint sprigs.

Yield: 4 burritos

Musakka'a Burrito

Once a semester, our college would sponsor "International Day" where students were encouraged to dress in native costume and prepare exotic meals for each other at a large outdoor festival on the Common. The most memorable meal, a delightfully rich Musakka'a casserole, was prepared by an Arabic student in the traditional manner; i.e., using copious quantities of olive oil (up to 10 cups!). I later attempted to duplicate the satisfying flavor using a fraction of the oil and came up with the recipe below. I decided to make it a burrito recipe since the tortilla would come in handy by absorbing all traces of oil from the eggplant.

15 oz. can garbanzo beans	3 large tomatoes, diced
1 large eggplant	¼ cup shelled pine nuts
½ cup vegetable oil	1 tsp. salt
1 large yellow onion, chopped	1 tsp. black pepper
	8 pita breads, warmed

Rinse and drain garbanzos in a sieve. Wash, stem, and cut eggplant into 1-inch cubes. Heat oil in large skillet on high heat; fry eggplant until it is tender, but not mushy. Remember to turn cubes so that eggplant cooks equally on all sides. Add onion, tomatoes, and garbanzos; fry, stirring frequently, until onion becomes soft and somewhat translucent. Add pine nuts and cook for 1 minute, stirring constantly. Pour skillet contents into large sieve so that oil can drain out into catchpan. Discard oil. Put contents back in skillet, making sure heat is off, and stir in seasonings; cover skillet to keep contents warm. Open a hole in pita breads by placing individual disks on board and carefully making an incision in the outer edge of each pita with a small serrated knife. Incision should be no longer than 3 inches. Carefully spoon eggplant mixture into pitas and serve immediately.

Yield: 8 pita burritos

NOTE: A problem with using pitas is that they cool off quickly. Try slitting pitas prior to cooking the filling, then stack and heat them in the oven wrapped in single sheet of aluminun foil. Stuffed pitas take microwave reheating very well.

Sun-Dried Tomato-Vegetable Burrito with Goat Cheese Crème

▼ ▼ ▼

Very Californian, this meatless burrito was inspired by Wolfgang Puck's famous ultra-pizzas served at Spago, Hollywood. Quick and easy, it offers endless variations.

▲ ▲ ▲

GOAT CHEESE CRÈME

8 oz. fresh goat cheese   1 cup crème fraîche

BURRITOS

1 small eggplant, diced   8 sun-dried tomatoes, sliced

6 green onions, chopped   2 tsp. Italian seasoning

1 zucchini, diced   2 Tb. white wine

2 small crookneck squash,   1 Tb. vegetable oil
  diced
                                 8 blue corn tortillas
12 button mushrooms, halved
                                 ½ cup chopped fresh
1 cup broccoli florets   coriander

8 artichoke hearts,   4 oz. crumbled feta cheese
  quartered
                                 Freshly ground black pepper

Combine ingredients in medium bowl to make a creamy mixture. Set aside.

Sauté vegetables with Italian seasoning in wine and oil until eggplant is tender and mushrooms turn golden brown. Place tortillas on board and spread with thick layer of goat cheese crème; reserve remaining crème. Portion sautéed vegetables equally among tortillas. Wrap tortillas jelly-roll style and place in casserole dish. Top with remaining crème, coriander, feta, and pepper.

Yield: 8 burritos, with 2 cups creme

Asparagus Cheese Burrito

▼ ▼ ▼

With lots of energizing carbohydrates, yet light on calories, these baked burritos have been likened by some to a primavera lasagne for dieters. Try substituting your favorite steamed vegetables for those listed for an easy variation. If raddichio is not available (or too expensive), red-leaf lettuce can take its place effectively.

▲ ▲ ▲

- 1 cup small curd low-fat cottage cheese
- 15 oz. can asparagus, drained and rinsed, or 1 cup steamed, chopped fresh
- 1 Tb. lemon juice
- 1 tsp. white pepper
- 1 tsp. Italian seasoning

- 1 grated carrot
- 1 medium Italian plum tomato, diced
- 1 small crookneck squash, thinly sliced
- 6 whole wheat tortillas
- 1 cup shredded raddichio

Preheat oven to 350 degrees.

In blender jar combine cottage cheese, asparagus, lemon juice, pepper, and Italian seasoning; blend until smooth, set aside. Lightly steam carrot, tomato, and squash (veggies should be fairly crisp). Apportion cheese mixture and steamed vegetables equally on tortillas. Top with raddichio. Fold tortillas in the classic style and place seam side down in baking dish. Cover with aluminum foil and bake for 20 minutes.

Yield: 8 burritos

VARIATION: Cooked frozen broccoli can be substituted for asparagus, just make sure it's drained well before blending.

Basic Breakfast Burrito

For those late mornings, here's a snappy breakfast to get you on your way. One pan makes for simple cleanup.

1 medium red onion, diced
⅓ cup butter
8 eggs, slightly beaten
½ tsp. chili powder
6 oz. can diced green chilies

¼ cup grated Parmesan cheese
Salt and pepper to taste
8 whole wheat tortillas

Preheat oven to 350 degrees.

Sauté onion in heated butter for 2 minutes. Add eggs, chili powder, and green chilies; scramble until eggs are firm but not dry. Turn off heat. Sprinkle Parmesan evenly over egg mixture, and add salt and pepper to taste; cover skillet to keep contents warm. Heat tortillas for 1 minute in microwave, or for 3 minutes in oven. Remove warm tortillas; spoon egg mixture evenly on tortillas. Wrap in classic style and serve immediately.

Yield: 8 burritos

VARIATIONS: Add a few drops of Tabasco sauce or ketchup to eggs. Substitute grated cheddar for Parmesan; add with green chilies and chili powder.

SAUCES AND SALSAS

▼▼▼

You can't always get everything you want *in* a burrito—sometimes it takes a little something *on* the burrito. So, now come the sauces.

Uncle Fred's Guacamole

▼▼▼

My uncle and his family immigrated to the sovereign state of Texas and immediately took to the local Mexican-inspired cuisine like ducks to water, particularly Fred. Nothing was better than steak tacos and beer (lotsa beer), and Fred loved to share this bounty with me and his son, Steven, when we were both little sprouts. 'Course, at that age, we didn't get much beer (at least, I didn't; Steven took to stealing sips when the "old man" was in the loo), but that jolly old bear of a man would more than make up for us. Eventually he'd dare one or both of us to drink from the salsa bottle, and trusting little tykes that we were, we did. Now this particular dusty café in Fort Stockton made some of the fiercest hot sauce around, but my tastebuds were created from cast iron and it didn't singe me a bit. Steven's buds were a little more sensitive and he'd have to cool them by sucking on ice cubes after about the sixth sip. Now, what does all this have to do with guacamole? Well, Fred would eventually take us back to the house and within an hour or so, he'd be missing some of that sizzling Mexican cuisine. So out would come whatever was in the fridge, and my favorite uncle would whip up something wonderful. 'Course, Steven and I were there to share like the greedy little beggars that we were. Fred didn't mind, and I idolized him for it.

▲ ▲ ▲

3 ripe avocados, peeled and pitted

3 tsp. lemon or lime juice

2 tsp. olive oil

½ tsp. salt

½ tsp. cayenne pepper

½ tsp. black pepper

1 hard-boiled egg, finely chopped

4 green onions, finely chopped

½ small green pepper, seeded and finely chopped

1 tomato, finely diced and drained

3 Serrano chilies, seeded and finely chopped

Splash of beer

In a large mixing bowl, mash the avocados with the lemon or lime juice until smooth. Add oil, salt, pepper, and egg, and mix thoroughly. Add onions, green pepper, tomato, chilies, and beer, stir well. Guacamole will be fairly thick and chunky. Serve with crisp tortilla chips, crackers, or celery stalks.

Yield: 2½–3 cups

Herbed Hollandaise Sauce

▼ ▼ ▼

Classic hollandaise is a bit of a pain to make from scratch, and it tends to curdle if the sauce gets a tad too hot during the cooking process, but the purchased variety is just not as tasty. So I encourage you to practice, practice, practice, while keeping in mind that it is an extremely versatile sauce suitable for a variety of burritos, such as fish, vegetarian, or breakfast style. Once you've mastered this version (and it may take some time), you can experiment with your own favorite seasonings and herbs, such as oregano, basil, rosemary, or whatever strikes your fancy. The helpful hints here come from Executive Chef Lou Gardella of the Poco Diablo Resort in Sedona, Arizona.

5 Tb. white wine vinegar	⅛ tsp. salt
6 peppercorns	⅛ tsp. tarragon
1 bay leaf	⅛ tsp. marjoram
¾ cup butter	⅛ tsp. lemon pepper
3 egg yolks	⅛ tsp. thyme

Boil vinegar, peppercorns, and bay leaf in small saucepan over medium-high heat. Once boiling, reduce heat to low and simmer about 10–12 minutes (mixture should reduce to a little more than 1 Tb.). Remove from heat and pour through a strainer into small bowl; discard peppercorns and bay leaf. In a separate small mixing bowl, hand whip the butter until it's smooth and airy. In a third bowl, beat the egg yolks, then add the salt and a heaping teaspoon of the whipped butter; beat together until smooth, then add vinegar and stir well. Fill a medium-size saucepan one-third full of warm (not hot) water. Lower the bowl with egg yolk mixture into the water, then place the pan over a very low heat. Stir constantly while the mixture thickens but do not let it come to a boil! Add the remaining butter while stirring constantly. Add tarragon, marjoram, lemon pepper, and thyme, stirring constantly. Remove from heat and use immediately.

Yield: about 1 cup

NOTE: If sauce is too pungent, add more butter. If sauce is too thick, add 1–2 tsp. light cream. If sauce curdles while cooking, immediately add 1–2 Tb. boiling water. If sauce is ready too soon, keep bowl half submerged in pan of hot (not boiling) water.

South-of-the-Border
Sour Cream Sauce

▼ ▼ ▼

A popular topping for wet-style burritos, or a smooth creamy binder for a variety of ingredients combined as a burrito filling. I particularly relish using this sauce for a shredded chicken, sliced sautéed mushrooms, and rice burrito.

▲ ▲ ▲

2 Tb. butter
1 small onion, finely diced
½ tsp. white or black pepper

¼ tsp. paprika or chili powder (for a spicier sauce)
1 cup dry white wine
1¼ cups sour cream

Melt butter over medium-high heat in medium saucepan; add onion, pepper, and paprika or chili powder. Fry about 8 minutes, stirring occasionally, until onion is golden brown. Stir in wine and simmer for 5 minutes, stirring once or twice, until wine is reduced by half. Remove pan from heat and stir in sour cream. Reduce heat to low and return pan to stove, cooking sauce 2–3 minutes, stirring constantly.

Yield: about 1 cup sauce, or enough for 6 burritos

Ranchera Sauce

▼ ▼ ▼

This is one of the most versatile sauces in Mexican or Southwest cuisine. This recipe comes from Barbara Klein (co-owner and executive chef of Serrano's restaurant in Sedona, Arizona), who enthuses: "This sauce is great over any burro! Topped with melted cheese, it's fabulous." Simple to make, luscious to enjoy, it takes minimal work for maximum results. If you can't find El Pato spicy tomato sauce in your grocery, try stopping by a Latin gourmet shop. If this fails, add 2 Tb. chili powder and 1 Tb. black pepper to regular tomato sauce for punch (remember to adjust amounts for your own comfort level). The whole peeled tomatoes can be chopped into 1-in. pieces by hand if a blender is not part of your kitchen array. The sauce can be stored in the freezer in an airtight container and thawed; it can also be stored in the refrigerator in a sealed container for approximately 1 week.

▲ ▲ ▲

Two **28-oz. cans whole peeled tomatoes**

Two **8-oz. cans El Pato "hot" tomato sauce**

Two **7-oz. cans diced green chilies, drained**

½ **tsp. garlic powder**

¼ **tsp. salt**

1 **large onion, chopped**

Place whole peeled tomatoes in blender jar and chop. Put all ingredients into a large pot and cook over a low heat for 2 hours, stirring occasionally.

Yield: about 6 cups

Spicy Guacamole

▼ ▼ ▼

Only for the brave—olé! Feel free to experiment with amounts and types of salsa and jalapeño peppers until you find your favorite recipe. Variations include adding splashes of Tabasco sauce, chopped tomatoes, fresh cilantro, or diced red onion. *Guaca* is from the Quecha language of Mexico and refers to something sacred, while *mole* is a type of sauce; guacamole therefore is an inspired sauce to be savored.

▲ ▲ ▲

4 **large ripe avocados, peeled and pitted**

½ **cup medium-hot red chili salsa**

⅓ **cup sliced pickled jalapeños**

2 **tsp. lemon juice**

In large mixing bowl, mash avocado until smooth. Add all ingredients, mixing well. Guacamole will be slightly lumpy due to jalapeño pieces.

Yield: 2 cups, or enough for 12–16 burritos

Quick Con Queso Sauce

▼ ▼ ▼

This sauce is served in seconds and makes a delicious addition to a plain chicken or beef burrito. For more zest, add chopped jalapeño peppers (available sliced in a can or bottle in grocery stores), then stir before pouring.

▲ ▲ ▲

8 oz. Mexican-style Velveta cheese spread	**2 Tb. milk** **½ cup green or red chili salsa**

In a saucepan, stir together cheese spread and milk over low heat until smooth; add salsa and stir well until thoroughly heated. Pour over burrito ingredients just prior to folding filled tortilla, or drizzle over top of folded burritos for "smothered" variety.

Yield: 1 cup

Gila Bend Salsa Verde

▼ ▼ ▼

A gila monster is a beautifully striped black and white lizard that grows up to 3 feet in length and has a lovely pebbly textured skin. It is also extremely poisonous and possesses a nasty temper. This Arizonan hot head is particularly prolific around a sleepy little town known as Gila Bend (as in, "there's a gila monster around every bend"). Back in the late seventies, I used to stop in a particular Mexican café (now closed, much to my ever-lasting sorrow) on my way to Fort Stockton, Texas, and indulge in whatever dish was christened with the hottest salsa verde I have ever tasted. Maria, the cook, finally agreed to part with her family recipe for the sauce, warning me that the heat varies with the strength and numbers of jalapeños used. I've adapted her recipe to suit tamer palates below; it is now a mild green sauce suitable for burritos, enchiladas, or as an addition to soup.

▲ ▲ ▲

12 oz. (about 12) tomatillos, peeled, washed, and quartered

1 cup chopped cilantro

6 green onions, chopped

4 cloves garlic, chopped

3 jalapeño peppers, chopped (remove seeds for less heat)

1 tsp. salt

1 tsp. sugar

1 cup water

Place all ingredients in medium pan and boil for 15 minutes. Pour contents of pan into a blender and puree until thick and smooth. Can be mixed with other burrito stuffings, or used as a pour-over garnish or sauce.

Yield: about 1 cup, or enough for 12 burritos

Basic Chicken Burrito Sauce

▼ ▼ ▼

What to do with leftover chicken breasts or turkey? Simply sauté some vegetables, add the warmed poultry, and pour on this delectable sauce for a quick and savory supper.

▲ ▲ ▲

2 Tb. butter

4 Tb. flour

2 cups chicken stock or canned chicken broth

2 tsp. vinegar

½ tsp. Dijon mustard

½ tsp. salt

¼ tsp. chili powder

¼ tsp. black pepper

2 Tb. light cream

Melt the butter over medium heat in a medium saucepan; stir in flour and continue cooking, stirring constantly, for 1 minute. Slowly pour in chicken stock or broth; continue stirring and add vinegar, mustard, salt, chili powder, and pepper. Increase heat slightly and bring to a boil, stirring constantly. When sauce is boiling, reduce heat to low and simmer for 5 minutes, stirring occasionally. Remove pan from heat and stir in the cream. Can be stored up to 4 days in refrigerator.

Yield: 2 cups, or enough for 12 hearty burritos

Homemade Tomato Sauce

▼ ▼ ▼

While canned sauce is readily available, it doesn't have the taste appeal of this simple-to-make, easy-to-store homemade variety. Almost every cook has favorite seasonings, so feel free to experiment until you find a winning combination.

▲ ▲ ▲

5 large, ripe tomatoes	1 tsp. butter
1 bay leaf	1 tsp. black pepper
1 tsp. thyme	1 tsp. sugar
1 tsp. garlic salt	1 tsp. basil

Wash tomatoes well; drain and quarter. Place tomatoes, bay leaf, thyme, and garlic salt in skillet; bring to a boil, stirring and crushing tomatoes with wooden spoon. Lower heat slightly and cook until tomatoes are thick and very pulpy. Remove from heat and let cool. Remove bay leaf. Run through a food mill or lacking that, place collander in large bowl; pour tomato mixture into collander and use the back of a wooden spoon or fingers to press tomatoes through until only skins and seeds are left. Pour pureed tomato back into skillet and discard remains. Add remaining ingredients and cook over medium heat until desired consistency is reached, stirring frequently to avoid burning. Remove from heat, let cool, and use as you would canned tomato sauce.

Yield: about 2 cups

NOTE: To thin sauce, add water by the tablespoon until desired consistency is reached.

Santa Fe Guacamole

▼ ▼ ▼

This is one of the more common, and most delicious, of mole recipes. It's served as an appetizer with a large basket of piping hot tortilla chips or as a garnish for spicy entrées in most New Mexican restaurants and homes. Many variations exist: those who can tolerate a lot of heat may wish to use jalapeño peppers instead of Serrano chilies; parsley may take the place of coriander or cilantro; fresh lemon juice can substitute for lime juice. Some recipes even add mayonnaise for smoother consistency. Experiment to find your favorite!

▲ ▲ ▲

1 Serrano chili

1 tsp. garlic paste

1 green onion, chopped

1 medium tomato, finely diced

3 medium ripe avocados

2 sprigs fresh cilantro, chopped

2 tsp. fresh lime juice

Salt to taste

Use a small knife or potato peeler to remove skin from Serrano chili; then seed and devein it. Finely dice chili and place in medium bowl; mash with back of wooden spoon until pulpy. Add garlic paste and mix well. Add onion and tomato and mash again. Split avocados, remove and discard pits; mash in separate bowl until creamy. Add avocado to chili mixture, mix well. Add cilantro, lime juice, and salt to taste; mix well and serve.

Yield: 2 cups

Mint Sauce

▼ ▼ ▼

Sure to add zest to a boring burrito, this sauce can be spooned over diced chicken and rice or slivered pork and red peppers prior to rolling up. Originally published in *The New American Vegetable Cookbook* (Aris Books, 1985), this sauce is easy to make but impossible to keep. Make sure to discard unused portion.

▲ ▲ ▲

2 jalapeño peppers

1 cup chopped fresh mint sprigs

2 Tb. rice wine vinegar

2 Tb. water

2 Tb. sugar

Seed, devein, and mince peppers. Place all ingredients in blender jar and puree until smooth. Serve at room temperature.

Yield: ½ cup

SAUCES
AND SALSAS

Updated Mole Sauce

It seems as though every family south of the border has a traditional mole recipe that's been handed down for generations. Mexican grandmothers jealously guard their secrets; if pressured to reveal their recipe, they often omit a small but vital ingredient that completely changes the subtle balance of flavors. This particular recipe is one I have created from the (very) general directions given to me by a Tucson homemaker. It's especially good with chicken, duck, turkey, or eggplant.

2 dried poblano chilies

2 cups canned chicken broth

2 cloves garlic

1 small onion, diced

3 Tb. vegetable oil

4 tomatillos, split in half

1 red bell pepper, chopped

1½ Tb. unsalted natural peanut butter

1 tsp. salt

1 blue corn tortilla, shredded

Toast chilies by placing them in a heavy skillet over high heat then pressing them with a wooden spoon for several minutes until they begin to soften. Do not let them change color, burn, or crisp! Remove after toasting and immediately place in 1 cup chicken broth; soak for 12 minutes. In the same skillet, cook garlic and onion in oil until onion is soft; add tomatillos skin side down, and continue cooking until onion is translucent, 2–3 minutes. Place chilies and broth and tomatillo mixture in blender jar; puree. Add remaining ingredients and blend until very smooth. Pour mole into skillet and simmer 5–7 minutes, stirring frequently. Finished mole sauce can be used inside burritos that are filled with beans and grains, but the preferable method is to drizzle the sauce over burritos to be enjoyed enchilada-style.

Yield: 2 cups

Tomatillo Salsa

From southern Texas comes this thick, medium hot salsa perfect for beef and pork burritos; can be served as a condiment or spread inside burritos. Tomatillos, also known as husk tomatoes, are bright green fruits about 1½ to 3 inches in diameter covered in a crinkly-sticky skin that is removed prior to utilization. Make sure to wash the tomatillos thoroughly after removing and discarding the husk, because there is a greasy residue.

6 tomatillos	1 clove garlic, minced
3 Hungarian wax chilies	½ cup chopped fresh cilantro
2 Serrano chilies	2 medium ripe avocados
3 Tb. chopped onion	1 tsp. lemon juice concentrate

Husk the tomatillos and boil whole for 6 minutes; drain and chop. Seed, devein, and dice chilies. In a small mixing bowl, combine tomatillos, onion, garlic, and cilantro with chilies. Peel and pit avocados. Add avocados and lemon juice concentrate to other ingredients. Mash until desired degree of chunkiness is achieved.

Yield: 2 cups

Salsa Cruda

This tangy, uncooked, common Mexican condiment is traditionally served with every meal. It's the perfect complement to burritos, enchiladas, or tacos. Whether it's spooned over the top of a burrito or used as part of the filling, it adds delightful punch. You can vary the amount of each ingredient quite a bit in order to create your favorite salsa.

6 large red tomatoes

1 medium white onion, diced

1 Tb. minced garlic

2 Serrano chilies

1 cup fresh chopped cilantro

2 Tb. water (optional)

Peel, seed, and chop the tomatoes into pieces no bigger than ½ in. Place in large mixing bowl with onion and garlic. Cut the tops off the chilies and discard. Split each chili in half lengthwise; remove and discard the seeds and fibers. Dice the chilies and add them and the cilantro to the tomato mixture; stir well. For a smoother relish, add water and stir vigorously to mash down the tomato pieces to desired consistency. Serve in bowl alongside burritos. To store, cover with plastic wrap and refrigerate; use within 2 days.

Yield: 2½–3 cups

Easy Guacamole

2 very ripe avocados

1 small onion diced

1 tsp. salt

1 tsp. black pepper

2 Tb. lemon juice

Peel avocados, discard pits, and mash pulp thoroughly in medium bowl. Add remaining ingredients and mix well. Serve immediately. (Avocado will darken if left at room temperature for more than 30 minutes).

Yield: 1 cup

SIDE DISHES

▼ ▼ ▼

By itself, a burrito is a wonderful thing, but like the rest of us, it benefits from a little company. Here are a few of my favorite burrito buddies.

East Meets Southwest Side

▼ ▼ ▼

This is an upscale variation of a side dish served at the almost-world-famous Tapiac's Take Out in East L.A. If you are willing to brave driving into this barrio, its dual Korean-Latino culinary heritage will yield many taste-temping rewards. Just make sure to park at the church across the street, especially if there is a wedding in progress. The picnic tables at the front of the restaurant yield an unsurpassed view of the colorful bridal party as it is photographed on the impressive stone steps, and will allow you to scout for thieves possibly wishing to steal your stereo. I, personally, have never had any trouble here and find both the personalities of the people and their muralistic wall art inspiring.

▲ ▲ ▲

2 cloves garlic, minced
8 tomatillos
½ tsp. cumin
½ tsp. black pepper
½ tsp. salt
½ cup sliced red onion

1 Tb. vegetable oil
¼ lb. shiitake mushrooms
¼ lb. straw mushrooms
½ lb. white button mushrooms
7 oz. can roasted green chilies, diced

Divide minced garlic in two equal parts. Husk tomatillos, wash thoroughly, slice into quarters, and place in blender jar. Add half the minced garlic, and the cumin, pepper, and salt; liquify.

Fry remaining minced garlic and onion slices in oil until onion is translucent. Add mushrooms and diced chilies, stirring carefully and constantly; cook until button mushrooms turn golden brown. Lower heat, add liquified mixture, and simmer 25–30 minutes.

Yield: 2 cups, 4 servings

Garbanzos Oaxacan Style Side

▼▼▼

This is a savory side dish that can also be utilized as a burrito filling when combined with a meat or marinated chicken breast. I've ordered this dish in many Mexican-American establishments throughout the Southwest, and have always been informed of its Oaxacan origins. Of course, I've cut down on prep time by using canned instead of cooked dried chick-peas (as garbanzos are known in some parts of the country).

▲▲▲

- 6 **slices bacon, cut into 1-in. pieces**
- 1 **medium red onion, finely diced**
- 1 **clove garlic, crushed**
- 2 **mild green chili peppers, seeded and diced**
- ½ **tsp. black pepper**
- ¼ **tsp. chili powder**
- ½ **cup canned tomato sauce**
- 10 **oz. can garbanzo beans, rinsed and drained**
- ¼ **cup finely chopped cilantro**

Fry bacon over medium-high heat in medium pan until just crispy. Add onion, garlic, and chili peppers, and continue frying, stirring occasionally, until onion is soft and almost translucent. Add pepper, chili powder, tomato sauce, and garbanzos, and stir well. Lower heat to medium and cook for 10 minutes; stir in cilantro and cook for 1 minute. Serve immediately.

Yield: 1½ cups, 4 servings

Fried Green Tomatoes

▼ ▼▼ ▼

A simple, and simply fabulous, side dish from Mexicali (also known as Calexico, depending which side of the U.S. border you stand on). At lunchtime you can walk through the side streets and watch street vendors cook on camp stove skillets. Usually eaten plain with grilled bread and a hunk of cheese, I've dressed up this dish with spices and Parmesan cheese. You use unripe tomatoes in this dish.

▲ ▲ ▲

4 large green tomatoes	1 tsp. fenugreek
3 Tb. butter	½ tsp. garlic salt
½ tsp. black pepper	4 Tb. grated Parmesan cheese

Preheat broiler.

Cut tomatoes into slices approximately ½ in. thick. Melt butter in large skillet; sauté tomatoes for 5 minutes, or until bubbly hot (do not overcook). Remove from heat and place in shallow baking pan or on cookie sheet. Mix spices in cup and sprinkle evenly on tomato slices. Top each slice with grated cheese. Broil for 1 minute on rack placed 2 in. below heating element (watch carefully that cheese does not blacken). Remove and serve immediately.

Yield: 4 servings

VARIATION: Substitute other herbs for fenugreek: ¼ tsp. basil combined with equal portions thyme and celery salt is tasty. Or use a slice of Meunster cheese instead of grated Parmesan under the broiler.

Mixed Grains Parmigiana

▼ ▼ ▼

Elsewhere in this book, I've stressed the importance of using a variety of rice and other grains for nutritional and varietal purposes, but what do you do with small quantities of leftover rice and grain? In the words of my Czech "nana" (grandmother), "Put zem in ze pot un cook!" The key here is to match grains by cooking times and water absorption.

▲ ▲ ▲

¼ cup barley groats
¼ cup wheat berries
¼ cup oat groats
¼ cup brown rice
1 cup chopped fresh parsley

1 cup grated Parmesan cheese
2 eggs, beaten
¼ cup milk
Butter

In medium pot, boil 1 cup water; add barley groats and wheat berries, cover, lower heat, and simmer for 60 minutes, or until grains are fairly tender (check consistency 45 minutes into cooking time). In a separate pot, boil 1 cup water; add oat groats and rice, cover, lower heat, and simmer 40–45 minutes, or until water is absorbed and grains are yielding. Combine cooked grains in large mixing bowl and stir in parsley and cheese.

Preheat oven to 300 degrees.

Beat eggs with milk; combine thoroughly with grain mixture. Pour mixture into heavily buttered 9-in.-square baking dish (nonstick should still be buttered), and bake on middle rack in oven 15–20 minutes, checking to see if grain is burning on bottom of pan.

Yield: 4–6 servings

Baked Cabbage

▼ ▼ ▼

The first culinary experience I can remember is watching my grandmother cook in a typical closet-sized, New York City apartment kitchen. Only 5 ft. tall, this Czechoslovakian thunderball did nothing short of working miracles with the often meager supplies that came her way.

This extremely quick, simple recipe makes a smashing side dish for many of the burrito recipes in this book. The variations are endless!

▲ ▲ ▲

1 large head green cabbage	1 tsp. black pepper
4 small red tomatoes, diced	⅛ tsp. cumin
1 small white onion, chopped	⅛ tsp. caraway seed
½ tsp. garlic powder	⅛ cup water or chicken stock
½ tsp. salt	

Preheat oven to 325 degrees.

Quarter the cabbage and boil it in a large pot for 10 minutes. Remove cabbage sections and place in a shallow baking dish. Combine other ingredients in small bowl and pour over cabbage. Bake for 30 minutes, or until liquid is absorbed. Turn cabbage pieces halfway through cooking time so top side does not overcook.

Yield: 4 servings

Oaxacan Cauliflower

▼ ▼ ▼

This is a wonderfully enchanting side dish to serve with virtually any type burrito—cauliflower has simply never tasted better!

▲ ▲ ▲

1 large cauliflower, broken into florets	2 corn tortillas, torn into 1-in. pieces
1 Tb. butter	¼ cup grated jalapeño jack cheese
1 large onion, sliced and pushed into rings	4 Tb. grated Parmesan cheese
1¼ cups tomato sauce	1 Tb. olive oil
1 tsp. chili powder	
¼ cup chopped cilantro	

Preheat oven to 425 degrees.

Boil cauliflower in pot until al dente (tender, but still firm); drain and set aside. Melt butter in large saucepan over medium heat; add onion and fry until soft and translucent. Add tomato sauce, chili powder, and cilantro, stirring until mixed well. Raise heat and bring mixture to a boil; add drained cauliflower and stir until all pieces are coated with sauce. Pour cauliflower-sauce mixture into baking dish; top with tortilla pieces. Add jack cheese, then sprinkle with Parmesan and olive oil. Place in preheated oven and bake for 15 minutes, or until Parmesan is golden brown. Remove and serve immediately.

Yield: 8 servings

Anaheim Chili Relish

▼ ▼ ▼

A favorite family-style condiment, this chunky relish is perfect for spooning into burritos, topping rice, or mixed into sweet corn kernels. The flavor is pungent rather than fiery, and of course if you choose to utilize another type of chili pepper for the relish, the resulting intensity will vary. This version is served almost everywhere in Baja, California.

▲ ▲ ▲

1 **clove garlic, crushed**

1 **medium onion, very finely chopped**

6 **medium tomatoes, finely diced**

6 **long green Anaheim chilies, seeded and finely chopped**

½ **tsp. salt**

½ **tsp. black pepper**

2 **Tb. vegetable or olive oil**

1 **Tb. cider or red wine vinegar**

Mix the garlic, onion, tomatoes, and chilies together in a medium mixing bowl. In a small bowl, mix together the salt, pepper, oil, and vinegar. Pour the oil-vinegar dressing over the tomato-chili mixture and stir well. Can be served immediately or covered and refrigerated.

Yield: about 2½–3 cups

Frijoles Negros

Black beans are a tasty alternative to refried bean filling and have a wonderfully firm, mealy texture with robust flavor. Notice that there is no lard in this recipe!

▲ ▲ ▲

- **2 cups dried black beans, soaked overnight**
- **1 clove garlic**
- **1 bay leaf**
- **½ tsp. salt**

- **1 large onion, diced**
- **2 celery stalks, chopped**
- **¼ tsp. cayenne pepper**

Put all ingredients in large pot in 6 cups water and boil for 10 minutes. Lower heat, cover pot, and simmer for approximately 1½ hours, or until beans are tender; add more water, if necessary, to keep beans covered. Remove garlic and bay leaf before using frijoles negros as a burrito filler. Beans should be whole and rather tender, not mushy.

Yield: 4–6 servings

VARIATION: Substitute chili powder for cayenne pepper for milder beans; ¼ cup dark rum can also be added for a more exotic flavor.

Gingered Adzuki Beans

▼ ▼ ▼

These Oriental-style beans are a perfect beginning for any Asian burrito. Add chopped bok choy, red cabbage, grated carrot, and slivered tofu for a health-conscious burrito wrapped in rice paper.

▲ ▲ ▲

2 cups dried adzuki beans	2 whole cloves
3 cups water	1 tsp. salt
1 clove garlic	1 onion, peeled
6 whole peppercorns	¼ cup plum jelly
1-in. piece fresh gingerroot	2 Tb. tamari
Two 1-in. pieces cinnamon stick	

Put half of the beans into a pot with 3 cups water and bring them to a boil. Put the garlic, peppercorns, gingerroot, cinnamon sticks, and cloves into a spice bag. Add the spice bag, the remaining beans, salt, and onion and bring mixture to a boil. After it reaches a full boil, cover and cook for about 2 hours, or until the beans are tender. Remove the onion and spice bag. Stir in the jelly and tamari. Beans are now ready to be used as burrito filling.

Yield: 4–6 servings

DESSERTS

▼ ▼ ▼

All good things—and meals—must come to an end, but there are (you guessed it) burritos for every occasion. And dessert is one of them.

Apple Burrito with Cheese

▼ ▼ ▼

One of the best things about my childhood summer vacations were the frequent jaunts the family would take up and down the eastern seaboard. I particularly loved going to Lake George, a placid retreat nestled amid the pines in upstate New York where we would splash away the day, then go into town for a bite. There used to be a sleepy little café that served home-style dinners and the most marvelous apple pie. Tart pippins packed the flaky crust and a thick wedge of cheddar slowly melted on top of the overly generous slice that I always managed to finish. More recently, the Oaxaca restaurant in Sedona, Arizona, reminded me of this childhood treat when they introduced a new dessert burrito (they call it a chimichanga) featuring the same contrasting flavors of that treasured pie. While Oaxaca's is deep-fried, the following recipe avoids the grease by baking this rich, sweet repast.

▲ ▲ ▲

7 pippin or Granny Smith apples
1 cup water
1 cup sugar

½ tsp. cinnamon
12 large flour tortillas
1 cup grated cheddar cheese

Peel, core, and slice the apples. Bring water, sugar, and cinnamon to a boil in medium pot. Add apples, lower heat, and simmer until apples are just tender (do not let them get mushy). Place catch pan under collander; drain apple mixture and save juice.

Preheat oven to 350 degrees.

Place tortillas on board; equally portion apples and cheddar cheese on each tortilla. Drizzle 2—3 tsp. of syrup over apples and cheese; fold each tortilla in classic style and place seam side down in lightly buttered shallow baking dish. Drizzle remaining syrup over burritos and bake 5—10 minutes, or until tortillas begin to crisp. Remove and serve immediately.

Yield: 12 burritos

VARIATION: Garnish with whipped cream and a sprinkle of cinnamon.

Fried Banana Dessert Burrito

▼ ▼ ▼

While flan is still the most requested dessert at Mexican restaurants, this sweet dénouemont is very popular throughout the Southwest and Mexico. Bananas should be very ripe (peel should be yellow with a few black spots).

▲ ▲ ▲

4 large ripe bananas	1 tsp. vanilla extract
⅓ cup unsalted butter	6 flour tortillas
½ cup sugar	4 Tb. vegetable oil
1 cup heavy cream	Ground cinnamon
¼ cup dark rum	

Peel and slice bananas into medium chunks. In large skillet, sauté bananas in butter until golden brown; drain and cool. Sprinkle with ¼ cup sugar and set aside. Whip cream until stiff; fold in remaining ¼ cup sugar, rum, and vanilla. Spread tortillas flat on board; portion banana chunks equally on each, creating an imaginary center line. Spoon whipped cream on top of banana chunks. Wrap burritos in pocket-square style.

In original skillet, heat oil until almost smoking. Using two spatulas, quickly fry burritos 1 or 2 at a time, turning them gently to make sure burrito skin turns crispy and light golden brown. Remove, blot with paper towel to get rid of excess oil. Sprinkle with cinnamon and serve immediately; garnish with any leftover cream if desired.

Yield: 6 burritos

VARIATION: Serve with scoop of vanilla ice cream à la mode.

Payson Pudding

▼▼▼

This "hasty" pudding was enjoyed by myself and guests of the Rim Institute in Payson, Arizona. The Rim puts on a series of seminars and lectures by leading New Age, spiritual, scientific, and philosophic speakers every summer in a large yurt. Situated on eight beautifully forested acres high on the Mogollon Rim, the institute's cuisine stems from volunteer staff who hail from around the world. During the last two years I have met with a shaman from Santa Fe, an Italian fresh from six months of living with the Huichol Indians of Northern Mexico, numerous yogis from all parts of India who led us through lovely dawn Sun Salutation exercises, a Nepalese monk, and an English mathematician who works out music derived from specific algebraic equations. This cultural stew yields a mostly vegetarian menu that can be created in minutes, yet is both tasty and nutritious.

▲▲▲

1 cup blue or yellow cornmeal (blue gives the best coloration)

3 cups purple grape juice, or dark raspberry or cranberry juice

1 cup plain yogurt

¼ cup honey (or more, depending on personal taste)

Combine cornmeal and juice in pot; stir constantly over low heat until very, very thick (about 10 minutes). Remove from heat and pour into blender or food processor; add yogurt and honey and blend on medium speed until creamy smooth. Pour into individual serving bowls or cups and refrigerate at least 2 hours.

Yield: 8 servings

Blue Corn Sopaipillas

▼ ▼ ▼

A classic fried bread prepared by many Native Americans, this recipe comes from an 87-year-old great-grandmother I met at Taos Pueblo in New Mexico, who prepares it daily in a tiny adobe room using a cast-iron skillet and primitive wood stove. Hearty and nourishing, the bread is not as light and fluffy as some other fried breads made only with wheat flour, but it possesses a superior taste and texture.

▲ ▲ ▲

2 cups blue cornmeal

2 cups white flour

4 tsp. baking powder

4 Tb. cinnamon sugar

About 1½ cups water

Oil for deep-frying

Powdered sugar

Wildflower or orange blossom honey

In a large bowl, mix together cornmeal, flour, baking powder, and cinnamon sugar. Add enough water to make a stiff dough. Flour a rolling pin (or spray with PAM) and roll out dough on lightly floured board to approximately ¼ in. thick but no thicker than ½ in. Cut rolled dough into circles with 3 in. diameter cookie cutter. Heat oil in skillet until it sputters, then fry sopaipillas one at a time, pushing them under the oil until they're golden brown and puffy on both sides (turn if necessary). Remove with tongs and drain well on paper towels. Sprinkle on powdered sugar, drizzle with honey, and serve piping hot.

Yield: 12–16 sopaipillas

Peruvian "Rice" Pudding

▼ ▼ ▼

Rice can be substituted for the quinoa, regular raisins can replace the golden (or they can be omitted entirely), and the amounts of sugar and cinnamon can be adjusted to taste. A friend adapted this recipe by adding grated lemon rind and diced candied apricot pieces! Obviously, everyone can have a little fun!

▲ ▲ ▲

1 cup quinoa, soaked in water for 30 minutes, drained

½ cup golden raisins, soaked in water for 30 minutes, drained

1¼ cups milk

1¼ cups heavy cream

¼ cup sugar

2 tsp. cinnamon

Combine all ingredients in top part of a double boiler. Fill the bottom halfway with water; cover top, place top into bottom, and put entire works over medium heat for 60 minutes, stirring occasionally, until quinoa is soft and most of liquid has been absorbed. Remove from heat, pour mixture into small serving dishes, and place in refrigerator to chill for at least 3 hours.

Yield: 4 servings

THE FINAL STEP: HOW TO EAT A BURRITO

▼▼▼

The one thing I haven't told you is how to eat a burrito. Think of a burrito as you would a sandwich or a piece of pizza; burritos are finger foods, designed to be consumed by using one's hands. Now there are some rather fastidious people who insist on knife and fork prior to savoring pizza; these same killjoys will most likely never indulge in picking up something as large as a burrito and plunging ahead without cutlery; however, one can always hope.

In general, the hard-and-fast rule is "If the burrito has been smothered in sauce or salsa or melted cheese, etc., use cutlery. If not, use your hands." Should you decide to enjoy eating burritos in the traditional, hand-held manner, there are a few things you should note:

1. Burritos may become bottom heavy, the forces of gravity (and fragility of tortillas) being what they are. Therefore, when initially lifting one's burrito from one's plate, please cup the left hand under the bottom end of the burrito to lend tender support while wrapping the right hand approximately 3 inches from the top of the burrito (this is for right-handed people; southpaws simply reverse the order).

2. Should the burrito be exceptionally saucy and in danger of leaking hot contents onto one's skin, a sheet of wax paper may be placed across the palm of the left hand prior to lifting the burrito. The edges of this sheet will automatically angle up,

forming a rough cup, and should be sufficient to hold any minor leaks while protecting one's hands.

3. If the burrito has sprung a leak that wax paper cannot hold, revert back to cutlery or wrap the burrito in a thin sheet of aluminum foil, peeling back the foil like a banana skin (2 inches at a time) as one consumes.

4. The first bite of the burrito is a bit like the first move in a chess game; it indicates a person's character. Some people bite into the burrito by ''attacking'' from either the right or left top corners; others simply pinch the top and shove the entire top third of the burrito into their mouths (children are notoriously ingenious at this technique). The idea is to keep as horizontal a line as possible across the now open top end to prevent content spillage and dripping.

5. Should spillage and dripping occur, it's time for a knife and fork again.

Essentially, that's all there is to it. Of course, you will find that as you practice conspicuous burrito consumption, you will slowly evolve your own best techniques. Like chopsticks, it takes practice to become adept. Do not become dismayed should your initial burrito encounter turn into something akin to a mud wrestling match; simply dip the corner of your napkin sedately into your glass of water, smile, clean up and grab a fork. Never admit defeat! Burritos are fun, fast, and easy food. So, just relax, eat, and enjoy.

Index